John Fishwick & Sons
1907 ~ 2007

A Century of Transport

author David Prescott

Front Cover Photographs:
Left - All Leyland PD2. Centre - Leyland PS2. Right - Leyland Olympic

Back Cover Photographs:
Top - Single Deckers during Centenary Year
Bottom left - Double Deckers during Centenary Year
Bottom right - Latest Tour Coach delivered 2007

Published by John Fishwick & Sons
Golden Hill Lane, Leyland PR25 3LE
Lancashire, England
www.fishwicks.co.uk

Foreword

Our great grandfather, John Fishwick, in 1907 moved to Leyland from Wales and started the business with a steam wagon with wooden spoke wheels fitted with steel tyres. He bought this lorry from a local company, The Lancashire Steam Motor Co., which later became Leyland Motors Ltd. Passenger services were introduced in 1911 when a second vehicle was purchased which was used for haulage during the week and converted for passenger carrying at weekends.

This side of the business grew steadily for the next two decades and by 1930 we were operating a network of stage carriage services between Leyland and Preston and the surrounding districts.

Haulage remained part of the business until 1951 when the fleet of lorries was sold to J. Canning and Sons Ltd. of Leyland.

In 1963 the opportunity arose to take over J. Singleton (Leyland) Ltd, a local coach operator which introduced us to coaches and excursion, private hire and tour operations.

This detailed book is almost a history of the British Motor Bus industry featuring mainly products from our once near neighbours, Leyland Motors. In recent years we have successfully adapted to the DAF products.

Our existence is a remarkable tribute to the many "characters", the Fishwick family and all of its staff who have given many years loyal service to applying the basic principles of providing a good quality service where buses never fail to operate and to the timetable, a policy which always has and continues to be our daily purpose.

Our own experiences (we have eighty years between us) have seen so many changes. Forty years ago we employed 100 drivers and conductors and had a big staff turnover due to the antisocial shift working patterns. It was not unusual to go round the houses very early in the morning trying to persuade people to come to work due to the failure of others to turn up for their shift. Now, thankfully, all conditions have improved considerably and many of our present staff have been with us for more than twenty years.

We are a forward looking company and have always taken every opportunity to embrace changing trends and technology, this being reflected in our fleet of vehicles and in our administration. With the assistance of Lancashire County Council we are now fully integrated into "Real Time" and shortly to encompass the complete workings of the "NOW" Card System which we anticipate could eventually eliminate cash handling.

We continue to operate in our traditional area with our buses in our long-standing two-tone green livery, representing the stability of our continued history.

We have to thank the people of Leyland and surrounding districts (many of whom are known personally to us at Fishwick's) for the support they have given us over many years. We know that they appreciate the unique and personal service that the Company and its staff pride themselves upon.

In recent years we have built up a considerable programme of luxury tours operated by a fleet of modern coaches operating throughout the U.K. and Europe. Our coaches are equipped with every modern facility with limited seating to afford maximum comfort. Our specialist drivers have all been with us for many years and take pride in the level of care provided to our clients.

May we thank everyone involved in their efforts to make our Centenary Celebrations a success, especially those who have voluntarily given up so much of their time. Special thanks must go to Bill Ashcroft who has begged, borrowed and cajoled anyone he knows (and some he doesn't) for sponsorship and any other help they felt able to give.

This book would not have been possible were it not for the considerable effort made by David Prescott who, as a regular visitor to our depot, has devoted many hours of research into its presentation. Well done and congratulations, David, your enthusiasm is remarkable and the book a credit to you.

John C. Brindle, MBE   James F. Hustler
Director   Director

Directors James Hustler left and John Brindle with two of the fleet
Leyland National 2, No7 - GCK 428W and
recent arrival DAF SB200/Plaxton Centro No25 - YJ07 JWE

Contents

Introduction

Very few transport-orientated companies have managed to operate under family control for as long as a century. However, in 2007 the bus and coach operator in Leyland, Lancashire namely John Fishwick & Sons achieved this status.

Mr. John Fishwick moved to the North West from Wales in search of work and after a short period as an employee at the Lancashire Steam Motor Company - LSMC, (becoming Leyland Motors in 1904) he set up his own haulage business with a LSMC steam wagon in 1907. By 1911 the established business, operated three vehicles, and Mr Fishwick saw an opportunity to provide a Saturday only passenger service to neighbouring town of Eccleston, converting one of the wagons for the purpose. (Can you imagine current legislation allowing this!)?

Both sides of the business prospered and in 1919 the first purpose built passenger carrying vehicle arrived. By the early 20's there were as many as eight operators in the area which created the first encounter of 'bus wars' for the company.

Both haulage and passenger services operated side by side until 1951. At this time it was decided to concentrate on passenger operation with the haulage side sold to one of the former drivers.

50 years on the vehicle strength consisted of 17 single and 16 double deck buses.

In 1963, the coach business and premises of J R Singletons, the bus operations having previously been taken over in 1935, were acquired and three new coaches purchased to cover the operations. Further diversification came in 1966 when the local body building firm of W H Fowler was acquired. With the larger bus operators monopolising the main body builders production this latest acquisition enabled the continued supply of bus bodies to the company and maintain its own repair facility.

In the early 80's it was an all Leyland fleet, operating Leopards, Atlanteans, Nationals and Tigers.

As a result of de-regulation in 1986, Fishwicks began Mini bus operations around Leyland, which ran until 2005.

The second encounter of 'bus wars' came in 1999, when another operator ran vehicles on the main Leyland to Preston route but were eventually unsuccessful, subsequently being taken over by Arriva.

The current fleet strength consists of 29 single, 7 double deck buses and 6 coaches. (+ d/l vehicle, 1 single deck).

The following pages will take the reader through the last century of John Fishwick & Sons, giving an insight into the vehicles, operations and family history of this fascinating operator.

David Prescott
Fulwood, Preston

July 2007

David Prescott with his restored Ribble coach

Chapter One
A Brief History of the Fleet
taken from John Fishwick & Sons 1907 - 1997

In 1907, Mr John Fishwick moved from Wales looking for work. After a short period working at the Lancashire Steam Motor Company, which later became Leyland Motors, he decided to start his own haulage business.

The first vehicle purchased was a LSMC wagon with spoke wooden wheels, fitted with steel tyres, and had a drop side type body. It was used for general haulage work around Leyland, hauling rubber from the local rubber works to Liverpool and Manchester. A top road speed of 8 mph, which was reduced to 5 mph when towing a trailer, was attained. Operations began from premises in Tuer Street, Leyland that it still occupies.

Expansion started in 1910 with the requirement for a second vehicle. Again it was a Leyland but this time an 'X' type Wagonette with a four-cylinder petrol engine. Initially used for local haulage work, however, the following year 1911, Mr Fishwick saw the opportunity of running a Saturday only passenger service to the local market in Leyland from Eccleston. Thus the current passenger service of today was launched, the conversion consisted of removing the flat platform body and installing a very basic bus type body, 36 seater charabanc, which had open sides with canvas curtains,

which buckled across for protection against the weather and a canvas roof. In wet weather, passengers travelled with their umbrellas up because other passengers travelling on the roof on the last departures from Preston on the Saturday night service had torn the canvas. Repairing the damaged roofs took hours during the following week which sometimes consisted of applying square patch advertisements to the inside roof for the passengers to see whilst travelling on their journey. The vehicle was considered to be quite 'posh' for the period. The fare between Eccleston and Preston via Leyland was 9d, (3p). The drivers named the vehicle 'The Old Rip'. In 1922 it conveyed passengers to the Preston Guild celebrations for one-shilling (5p) per return trip.

Towards the middle of that year a second 'X' type wagon arrived with platform body and cab. The fourth vehicle came in early 1913 which was a Leyland X3 complete with bus body and was named 'The Hanley'. It is believed that both the previous vehicles were commondered for war duties in 1914.

By 1914 a further 'X' type, this time an X4 arrived which also performed dual duties, i.e. passenger duties as well as haulage work which also necessitated

The first vehicle operated by John Fishwick was a Steam Wagon

B5783 one of the Leyland 'X' Type wagons, seen here at Rhyl. The vehicle was converted at weekends with a removable bus body to carry passengers to Preston or for other trips.

changing bodies when required. Although the passenger body was a little more sophisticated having full width leather seats and a canvas roof which folded away behind the rear seat. The permitted maximum top speed was 12 mph, this vehicle attained 45 mph, and was therefore used for trips to Wales or pub outings besides the local runs. Again given a name - '"The May Queen" or "The Queen Mary". During the 1914 -18 war it is believed to have been converted and used as a fire engine.

During the war nearly all vehicle production was diverted to the armed forces. The only vehicle purchased during this period was a Leyland RAF type wagon (known as a subsidy wagon), primarily for haulage work but it also doubled as a bus using the body from 'The Hanley'. Throughout the war, John Fishwick assisted by two of his sons, operated both the haulage and the now regular bus services and

maintained vehicles. After the war the RAF type subsidy wagons became commercially available, a second one was purchased which operated on the haulage side of the business.

As vehicles became more available, the first purpose-built bus was purchased, in 1919, a Leyland S5 or 'N' type complete with a 20-seat Leyland body and featured acetylene lamps and solid tyre wheels. The bodywork had windows all round, including a driver's front screen, and had front and rear nearside entrance/exit via fixed external steps. Four more similar type vehicles joined the fleet between 1920 and 1922. Regular but non-timetable service runs were being operated from Leyland and the surrounding districts to Preston and Chorley as well as a special service to Ormskirk on the Thursday market days. The first authorised operators, by Leyland Council in 1920, to run services from Leyland to Preston were Bridges and Fishwicks.

In 1921 a new vehicle licensing system was introduced. Vehicles registered prior to the change retained their original registration marks. The registration marks of vehicles not re-registered, and vehicles which had been scrapped, were voided and subsequently re-used, possibly on a different type of vehicle.

With increasing competition from other local operators on the main route to Preston, Fishwicks,

The first RAF subsidy vehicle B5951 seen here with a hooped frame - flat bed body for haulage work

Ribble and Bridges joined together to form "The Leyland Motor Bus Service", Fishwicks and Bridges being two of the local operators authorised by Leyland council to operate the services. By 1922, the two local operators were providing as many as 130 trips a week with Ribble providing as many again. The joint operation lasted until the middle of 1927 when a newly formed operator, The Yarrow Motor Company, purchased the Bridges Bus business. Competition between the remaining local operators continued for some time. The drivers raced between stops to pick up as many passengers as they could. Very often the vehicles were overloaded and many mishaps occurred such as smoke and steam being emitted from under the bonnet. In the end, Fishwicks who had purchased four vehicles specifically for the job, in late 1923 and early 1924 won the race. They were the first in the fleet to have nap-pneumatic tyres. The livery was pale green, which was the colour favoured at this time for the bus fleet. The vehicles were based on the Leyland A9 chassis and the body was based on the "Chester" style with front entrance and twenty seats. The vehicles were known as "whippets", probably because of their speed and comfort in comparison to most other vehicles around at the time.

On the haulage side in 1924, a new wagon was also purchased, based on a Leyland SQH2 chassis having a long wheelbase and featured semi-forward control cab and bodywork of flat platform with a headboard. Wagons of this period were not as advanced as buses, still having solid tyres and spoked wheels. At about this time, the wagon fleet began to take on a different image being painted dark red, (damson).

By the mid twenties competition by local independent operators had increased to as many as eight. The most successful were Singletons, Dallas and Fishwicks; the latter two being the largest.

In late 1925, Leyland introduced a new model of bus with forward-control called the "Lion". Fishwicks bought their first two examples in March 1926 but had some difficulty in registering them for service with the local licensing authority in Preston. One of the vehicles was used, prior to delivery to Fishwicks, as a demonstrator. The vehicles first appeared in the local May festival procession. They were based on the short wheelbase version PLSC1 Leyland Lion chassis, (the 'P' denoting pneumatic tyres). The bodies were also made by Leyland and had front entrances and electric lighting. The livery prior to delivery of these vehicles was basically pale green, with black lining to emphasise the bodylines. The name "FISHWICKS MOTOR SERVICES" appeared along each side on the new buses along with the telephone number - 7 - at the same level across the rear panel. (It is interesting to note that last digit of the present telephone number is 7 - i.e. 421207). Several changes to the livery were introduced on these new Lions. They included a dark green waistband below the windows which carried a revised fleet name of 'J. FISHWICK & SONS', ivory roofs and black mudguards.

No15 - TE4622. A 1928 Leyland Lion PLSC3, one of thirteen operated by the company, seen climbing over the southern of the two adjacent rail bridges in Lostock Hall on its way to Preston.

Chapter One - JOHN FISHWICK & SONS 1907 - 2007

Over the next two years, the haulage side of the business continued to expand with the addition of three new vehicles. The first was based on a Leyland QH2 chassis followed by another Leyland SQ type vehicle and finally a special SWQ2 which differed from the previous two in that it had a third axle with outward facing wheels. Having a third axle meant that it could carry much more weight and proved to be more reliable operating for almost twenty years.

The number of Passenger licences held was 24, which was an increase over the 1926 figure of 50% when only 16 were held.

By this time, 1927, approximately 20 years after the company was formed, the fleet comprised of 18 vehicles, as follows:

7 wagons	I x Leyland X4
	2 x Leyland RAF - subsidy
	I x Leyland SQ2
	I x Leyland SWQ2
	I x Leyland SQH2
	I x Leyland QH2
I I single deck buses	5 x Leyland S5
	4 x Leyland A9
	2 x Leyland Lion PLSC I

Expansion of the bus fleet continued over the following years. In 1927 more Leyland Lions, this time the long wheelbase type, (PLSC3). Seven in all arrived over that year, one had apparently been ordered by another local operator, Parkinsons. This reflected, again, the increasing numbers of passengers and expansion of routes. The vehicle numbering system changed slightly, instead of consecutive numbers for both wagons and buses, each then proceeded to take the next consecutive number for the vehicle type, bus or wagon. Four more Leyland Lion PLSC3's arrived in late June1928. The price of the PLSC3 was around £1564 compared to £1278 for the PLSC1.

Another multiple intake of new vehicles came in 1929, in the form of five Leyland TS2 single-deck buses known as 'Tigers' with Leyland 33-seat, front entrance bodywork. Engine size increased to a six cylinder, 6.8-litre (38.9hp) from the four-cylinder, 5.1-litre (28.9 hp) used in the Lions, reflecting the price increase to £1800. Only one, No 14, received 8.6-litre Oil (diesel) engine, when they became available after the war in 1946. No 12, on the other hand, had the distinction of being the first ever-motorised passenger vehicle to climb over the Kirkstone Pass in the Lake District. After the initial trip, several of the other Tigers followed the same route on weekend excursions, sometimes in convoy. By this time

stage carriage services had progressively increased and frequency of operation operating at less than 10 minutes on a Saturday. The area being covered included several routes to Preston, Chorley, Bamber Bridge and Ormskirk. These vehicles were the first to be fitted with a special sign at the top of the forward facing near-side window, which read J. FISHWICKS and was in pale green. When the internal lights were illuminated, the passengers could see from a distance that it was a Fishwick vehicle approaching. The signs also appeared on the TD1, TD4 and TD5 vehicles in the lower deck front windows.

In 1930, the Road Traffic Act was passed. This meant that Licence applications had to be made to the Chorley Commissioners for the various routes. Fishwicks were successful in obtaining the following: -

Preston	to Earnshaw Bridge	via Leyland
Preston	to Moss Side	via Earnshaw Bridge
Preston	to Bent Bridge	via Leyland
Preston	to Eccleston	via Leyland
Moss Side	to Chorley	via Leyland
Earnshaw Bridge	to Bamber Bridge (Sunday Only)	via Leyland
Leyland	to Ormskirk	Two Routes

A considerable number of workmen's and church services were also operated.

Also that year, some South of Leyland licences, were exchanged for four vehicles with Yarrows. Two were PLSCl's which had originated from the Eccleston Motor Bus Company and Bridges, before take-over by Yarrows. The other two were PLSC3's and were originally new to Yarrows. In 1934/5, Fishwicks converted one of them to a wagon. The original clutch, radiator, transmission and rear axle were all retained, against advice, (but William Fishwick maintained that if the clutch could withstand bus work it would be OK for haulage. With the absence of any trouble in that area, he was proved to be correct). Stronger road springs were fitted and the unladen weight with platform body was reduced to 3 tons 19 1/2 cwt from 4 tons 8 1/4 cwt. It was mainly used to carry 5 tons of cotton bales every day, except Sunday, between a local mill and Manchester. It operated with Fishwicks until the early 1950's when it was sold with the haulage business, although it was never operated by the new owner.

Altogether some seventeen PLSC type Leyland Lions were operated by Fishwicks of which at least ten were in service for between 18 and 23 years, the last leaving the fleet in 1951. By this time fleet strength was up to 20 vehicles employing a staff of 60.

The first double deck buses arrived in June 1931, in the form of three Leyland Titan TDl's Leyland lowbridge 51-seat rear entrance bodywork. Originally fitted with six-cylinder petrol engines all received 8.6-litre diesel engines after the war. During the war, the liveries of numbers 1 and 3 was changed from light green to grey, the dark green band above the lower deck windows was retained along with the name "J. FISHWICK & SONS" down each side. By the time they were withdrawn they almost certainly would have completed 1,000,000 miles in service with Fishwicks.

Vehicles purchased in late 1933, early 1934 were for the haulage side of the fleet in the form of three Leyland Beaver TSC9's and a Leyland Bull TSQ3 (first registered in 1932 as a demonstration vehicle). All had platform type body work and six-cylinder oil (diesel) engines. Three Dyson four wheel draw-bar trailers were used with the Beavers. During the war, everything was carried; petrol in jerry cans, tinned milk between Preston and Lancaster, tea, tinned fruit to Blackburn, tent poles, tents, wood pulp, tyres, rubber and carbon black for BTR (British Tyre and Rubber Company, a local company based in Leyland), and even bacon from Cardiff.

One of the most competitive routes had been Preston to Leyland although by 1935 was down to four local operators. However on 18th August 1935, the stage carriage operations of two - Parkinsons and Singletons were jointly taken over by the other two Fishwicks and Ribble. A pooling arrangement was set up with Ribble on all services to, from, and through Leyland. It differed from other agreements set up by Ribble in that Fishwicks was the major partner, having a two-thirds interest. The agreement continued until de-regulation in 1986. This take-over meant that all the local opposition had finally disappeared and that Fishwicks was the only remaining independent operator in the area. The business continued to expand, with emphasis on the stage carriage side.

At the end of 1935 three Leyland Titan TD4 with Leyland wood frame/Burlingham lowbridge double deck vehicles entered service.

They were followed by four Leyland Titan TD5's with Burlingham low bridge double deck metal bodies at the end of June 1937, number 21 being the first to arrive. All initially had six cylinder petrol engines until after the war when they were replaced with diesel

ATD774 – No4. One of the three Leyland Titan TD4's with Leyland / Burlingham bodywork, seen leaving Fox street bus station.

engines. Altogether, ten buses were converted from petrol to diesel engines, which prolonged service for up to twenty-two years on some of these vehicles. Being on the doorstep of the Leyland factories many services to the outlying areas for the workers were being operated by Fishwicks.

The last vehicles to be purchased prior to the outbreak of war arrived in January 1939. They were four Leyland Lion LT9's with Leyland 35 bus seat, front entrance, single deck bodywork and four cylinder, 5.9-litre petrol engines. During the war, the War Department commandeered one. At least four of the other vehicles were painted in wartime grey, also one of the PLSC Lions was converted to an ambulance in dark blue.

On 1 April 1939, the services of the Yarrow Bus Company of Eccleston were jointly acquired with Ribble. None of the Yarrow vehicles were absorbed into either fleet. Fishwick vehicles then began working through to Wigan via Eccleston. As a result of this take-

Leyland Tiger PS1 GTE395 – No11 with Burlingham bodywork new in 1947, crossing Fishergate Hill Railway station bridge, Preston

maintained or overhauled by W H Fowler, a local coachbuilding firm which features strongly in the story's later years. Average mileage of the Lion buses by this time was 613000 miles and one of the Titan TD1's had completed 750000 miles, running on many of the original parts.

over, Fishwicks emerged as the only remaining 'small operator' in the area. During the war years, the operating services were drastically cut; even the peak hour services were affected, priority being given to the movement of workers to and from the local factories. These were, of course, Ministry of Supply factories, which were producing military vehicles and munitions for the war effort. However, records show that it was still a busy time. By this time over half the fleet was more than ten years old although the bodywork was considered to be in pristine condition having been

After the war normal operation was resumed with priority still concentrating on giving top service to the local industry with a large commitment of vehicles to peak hour services, resulting in busier times allowing rebuild of the fleet to be undertaken. Also the first of the three new garages was built. The first vehicles to arrive, in 1946, were two Leyland Tiger PS1 single deck buses with Burlingham bodies with six-cylinder, 7.4-litre diesel engines fitted from new. Two more double deck vehicles also arrived that year in the form of Leyland Titan PD1s with Leyland lowbridge bodies. A further two single Decker's, similar to the previous type arrived autumn the following year.

A review of the fleet, 40 years after the company was founded, showed the fleet to consist of some 37 vehicles, comprised as follows:

No33 - GTF283. One of two Leyland Titan PD1A's with Leyland lowbridge bodywork seen opposite Leyland Police station on the main route to Preston.

4 wagons	1 x Leyland Lion PLSC – con
	3 x Leyland Beaver TSC9
21 single deck buses	8 x Leyland Lion PLSC
	5 x Leyland Tiger TS2
	4 x Leyland Lion LT9
	2 x Leyland Tiger PS1
17 double deck buses	3 x Leyland Titan TD1
	3 x Leyland Titan TD4
	4 x Leyland Titan TD5
	2 x Leyland Titan PD1

In 1949 with the increasing passenger loading, two "off the shelf" - stock vehicles were purchased, they were Leyland Titan PD2/1s with 7ft 6in wide Leyland highbridge bodies with open rear entrances. The engine size had been increased to 9.8 litres and they had moquette seats instead of the usual leather type. Later in the year another two Leyland Tiger PS1's again with Burlingham bodies were also purchased bringing the total of this type to six.

Over the next few years, 1950/1, four Leyland Titan PD2/1 arrived. The first had 7ft 6in wide Leyland lowbridge bodywork with an open rear entrance and the next three 8 feet wide bodies. (Permitted by a change in the regulations in 1951).

The former one, No. 23, was fitted with a different axle ratio, and was reported to be much faster at climbing the Pear Tree Brow hill on the main Preston to Leyland route thus being favoured more by the drivers and worked harder than other buses.

No 23 - LTD445. Seen in Hough Lane operating on the Croston Road route to Preston, now the 115 route.

A new era of single deck buses started in 1951 with the arrival of eight Leyland / MCW Olympics. These were integral vehicles, (i.e. chassis-less), with Leyland

running units. Two were fitted with 40-semi coach seating and the other six had 44 standard seats. As they also had the 9.8 litre engine, with the lightweight body, they ran for up to twenty-one years. Over the previous 12 months, a total of twelve new buses were delivered. Also that year, one of the drivers decided to start his own haulage business under the name of J Canning and

View from back yard of 124 Golden Hill Lane of the new office block, shortly after construction in 1952. Refurbished between 1994 and 1996

Sons, which ended Fishwicks involvement in the general haulage business. Up to 10 `A' Licences were held by Fishwicks, over the 43 years of haulage operations. The maximum strength of haulage side only reached 10 wagons, employing 12 men.

Just over two and a half years elapsed, before the next new buses arrived in 1954, which were two more Leyland Titan PD2`s which differed from the previous deliveries by having a slightly longer wheelbase and Leyland highbridge 56 seat bodies. They proved to be the last Leyland bodies to be acquired as Leyland ceased production of bus bodies at around that time.

The next new vehicles, some twelve in all, arrived late 1957 and early 1958. The first were six single deck Leyland Olympians, which were the lighter version of the Olympic, having a smaller engine, which possibly was the reason that total production of this type was only in the region of 60-65 vehicles. In 1964 two were re-furbished to coach specification joining the expanding coach side of the business (see lower down the page) returning to stage carriage work in 1968. One example of this batch type has returned to home ground, Leyland, and has been fully restored and is now back in full Fishwick livery.

Two examples of the six 1958 Leyland PD2/40's with Weymann lowbridge bodywork after rear door conversion completed. Nos. 4 & 21 – 527 / 532CTF

The Olympians were followed by six Leyland PD2/40's with MCW lowbridge aluminium bodies. On delivery they had open rear entrances but were fitted with rear manually operated doors after a few years. One remained in the fleet for twenty years being used latterly on driver training duties, as, by this time, it was the only double deck vehicle with a manual gearbox. After spending nearly fourteen years away from Leyland, it returned and is now fully restored in full Fishwick livery. Both these preserved vehicles are frequently seen at vintage events.

By this time, over 9000 passengers were being carried daily. Total overall passengers carried in 1957 were 6,302,269. General repairs and maintenance work was carried out in the Company's own workshops.

One of John Fishwick's requests was that the bus livery, of two shades of green, be maintained as long as operation by the family continued. This has basically been maintained with only slight changes over the years, to layout / application of the two shades and latterly the addition of a gold stripe.

Some six years on, in 1963, the company employed 115 and weekly mileage was in the region of 24,000 miles over the 44 vehicles, carrying 80,000 passengers.

Another era began on 23rd June 1963 with the acquisition of J R Singleton's, (established 1872 with horse drawn traps and hearse), and completing the take-

over that started in 1935. A mutual agreement was struck allowing both companies to progress their relevant fields, i.e. Fishwicks in passenger carriage and Singletons in haulage. Fishwicks retained the excursion and private hire licences, as well as the booking office in the centre of Leyland, but the coaches were sold. A new garage was built, which had space for ten vehicles and a wash bay. The new premises also doubled as a coach station, opening 14th November 1965, which incorporated a waiting room with vending machine for refreshments, access being from the booking office. Three new coaches were purchased a Leyland L type Leopard and two Albion Victors, all with Duple Dragonfly and Firefly bodies. As this was a new side to the business a new livery was introduced which consisted of a deep waistband in Guildford Blue and the remainder was in Arundel Grey. Fleetnames were only carried on the rear boot panels. A new numbering system for coaches was started which included a 'C' prefix. A second example of the Dragonfly bodied Leopard was purchased in 1966, having been used by Leyland as a demonstrator and by the Sports and Social Club for outings. Only six Dragonfly bodies were built by Duple, Fishwicks operated two of them. The intake of the two Albions was the first deviation from an all Leyland fleet, which had lasted some 56 years.

Later in 1963 the first examples of the new breed of double deck buses arrived. They were four Leyland Atlantean PDRl/l's which had 73-seat lowbridge MCW bodywork, (built by Weymann). Four more similar vehicles were purchased over the next three years, one in early 1964 followed by three in mid 1966 all having the bodies mainly built by MCW. Two of them were exported to Victoria BC - Vancouver Island in Canada

One of two Albion Victor coaches with Duple Firefly bodywork purchased to launch the coach business in 1963 was C3 – 7589TF

The third vehicle to receive fleet No. 23 was one of the Leyland Atlantean PDR1/1 Mk11 with Weymann lowbridge bodywork new in 1964. CTE442B

where they operated as tour buses. No 35 was seen on 16th June 1996 in Victoria supporting 'Oak Bay Explorer' livery. The upper deck was still to the original seating layout, but the lower deck had been modified to accommodate the additional drivers side entrance door. They were operated by Grayline West, and still carried the Fishwick's registration, fleet number plates and even the original destination blinds displaying 'COPPULL, STANDISH and PNE / ST. MARY'S CHURCH'. (On contacting the company, I believe they ran up to last year, one is still owned but not being used this year and the other has now been sold to a Christian Group in Vancouver).

The fourth new coach to be purchased was this 1965 Leyland Leopard PSU3 with Duple Commander bodywork. C6 – RTD432C

In January 1964, to help cope with the increasing passenger numbers on the Preston - Leyland - Chorley route, two 36ft long Leyland Leopard PSU3 single deck buses were purchased. The bodywork was again MCW built by Weymann. They had 49 seats which was as many as some of the early double deck vehicles used to seat. Single deck buses were required on this route as a low, narrow railway bridge restricted it.

The first year of coach operation proved to be very successful which resulted in the need for more vehicles at certain times. It was decided that two of the Leyland Olympians were to be overhauled mechanically and sent to Duple Coachbuilders at Blackpool for the bodies to be modernised and re-styled. The cost of the refurbishing was between £1000 and £1500 per vehicle, which included repainting into the new coach livery. They operated in the coach fleet until 1968 when they returned to stage carriage duties and repainted in bus livery the following year.

Back to 1965 which saw the arrival of three completely different vehicles, a Leyland Atlantean and two Leyland Leopards. The Atlantean was the second of what proved to be many ex-demonstration vehicles purchased by Fishwicks. It had Alexander highbridge bodywork, being originally built for Glasgow Corporation Transport in 1962. The first of the Leopards was for the coach fleet. It had a Duple Commander body, the chassis type was PSU3/4R which included the larger 11.1-litre engine. The second Leopard had a dual-purpose MCW body, (built by Weymann), with coach type leather seats and painted in the bus livery. It ceased dual-purpose duties after a relatively short period, just over three years, but continued on normal stage carriage operation for a further twelve years until 1981.

Leyland Leopards were favoured for the coach fleet for the

Also in 1965 came a Leyland Leopard PSU3 with Weymann dual purpose bodywork seen on private hire work at unknown location. No33 - STC359C

the 1970's, with long delivery times from the large body-builders, (major fleet operators being given preference), Fishwicks decided to design and build their own bodies at the Fowler premises. Other vehicle deliveries that year were a midi coach for the still expanding coach fleet which was a Bedford J2 with a Duple 20-seat body, also being the first non-Leyland Group vehicle to be purchased. Two single deck buses also arrived at the later end, which had Leyland Tiger Cub PSUC chassis with bodies by Massey of Wigan.

The next year 1967, only one vehicle was purchased for the coach side. It was an Austin 1600cc with a Fineline Walker's of Watford, twelve-seat body. Also that year the stage carriage fares increased, examples:

Single from Leyland Cross to Preston rose by 1d to 1s 6d
Return by 2d to 2s 11d.

A typical days running duty of double deck vehicle in 1967 would be: -

	Oil and water check by garage staff
0615	Leyland Motors North Works to Tithebarn Street bus station Preston (night shift workers)
0645	Tithebarn Street to various factories around Leyland, then double back for
0715	Tardy Gate to Leyland Motors North and South Works via Golden Hill Lane
0739	Earnshaw Bridge to Preston Fox Street via Leyland, Lostock Hall and Lower Penwortham
0817	Fox Street to Leyland Motors South Works via Lostock Hall and Golden Hill Lane (office workers)
	Proceeding to Leyland Cross to carry school children from connecting Wigan service to local grammar school
0846	Bent bridge to three local primary schools in Leyland Farrington area
	Returning to garage for fuel, oil checks and cleaning. New crew
	Two runs Black Bull Hotel, Midge Hall Preston Fox Street to Preston Fox Street via Croston Road arriving 1509
1515	Preston Fox Street to Leyland then returning to garage for another new crew
	From local secondary school to Charnock Richard then returning to garage for another new crew
1705	Local works service to Preston
	Returning on a duplicate service to Black Bull Hotel (office and shop workers)
1815	Leyland Motors South Works via North Works and Golden Hill Lane to Tithebarn Street bus station Preston
1910	Tithebarn Street to various factories around Leyland (night shift workers). Last run of day
	Returning to garage for cleaning ready for next day's duties.

next fifteen years with either Duple or Plaxton bodies. The first of these, in 1966, was a PSU4/4R model with a Leyland 680 (11.1-litre) engine and a 41 seat Plaxton Panorama body. It was the first of this type, a short Leopard, to be fitted with a 680 engine.

Yearly figures to the end of March 1966 saw around 5500000 passengers carried by the buses and coaches over 1300000 miles.

J. FISHWICK & SONS
TRAVEL AGENCY

AND
COACH STATION

FISHWICK

11 CHAPEL BROW, LEYLAND
Telephone 21207 and 21264

A mid 60's brochure showing the travel agency front in Chapel Brow fronting the coach garage acquired from Singletons

Another milestone came in August 1966 with the acquisition of local bodybuilders, WH Fowler's, following the death of the remaining partner. The firm was founded in 1926 by two brothers, manufacturing mainly wagon bodies. One of the conditions of the sale to Fishwicks was that the business should continue to trade under the Fowler name for a certain period. The Fishwicks name finally appeared over the premises in Hastings Road, Leyland in 1975. After take-over, the outside business was wound down in favour of repair and repaint work on the Fishwick fleet vehicles. Then, at the beginning of

By January 1967, number 5, one of the Leyland PD2 /MCW bodied, 58 seat double deck buses had covered 412000 miles. First and only engine overhaul undertaken in December 1964 after 249490 miles.

The number of employees, by this time, had risen to 200 and the company prided itself with their labour relations as there had been no disputes over all the years it had been operating.

The fleet strength after sixty years, in mid 1967, was a total of 44 vehicles, (all passenger vehicles), comprised as follows:

17 single deck buses	2 x Leyland Tiger Cub
	4 x Leyland Olympian
	8 x Leyland Olympic
	2 x Leyland Leopard
	I x Leyland Leopard DP
17 double deck buses	8 x Leyland Titan PD2
	9 x Leyland Atlantean PDRI/I
10 coaches	2 x Albion Victor
	4 x Leyland Leopard
	2 x Leyland Olympian - DP
	I x Bedford – midi
	I x Austin - mini

The first Fishwicks vehicle to emerge from the Fowler bodybuilder was another mini bus. It was based on a Ford Transit chassis, which was delivered in March 1968. The bodywork took just over four months to complete. It was fitted with twelve coach type seats, and entered service in August 1968. A new Transport Bill was also introduced that year which was to have widespread and far-reaching effects on all operators, large and small. Excursions in that year were advertised as follows:

	adult	child
Blackpool	4/6d	3/-
Morecambe	5/9d	4/-

The following year, 1969, saw the arrival of another ex-demonstration vehicle, which had been built the previous year. It was a Leyland Panther PSUR1/1R with single deck Park Royal bodywork incorporating dual-door layout, which was later converted by the body shop, (Fowlers), to single door although no additional seats were fitted. On receiving fleet colours a slight change to the livery layout was used which consisted of the dark green being extended to completely surround the windows.

All subsequent new vehicles and repaints received this revised livery, only applying to the lower deck on double deck vehicles.

Also in 1969, the new central bus station in Preston was completed. It was built on the sites of the old Ribble bus and coach stations in Tithebarn Street and North Road. When opened it was acclaimed as being the largest bus station in Europe. In October 1969, Fishwicks began operating all their Preston services from four stands of the new bus station. Their Fox Street bus station, which had five stands and a small waiting room, was eventually sold to the Post Office, which had a Delivery Office next door. More recently it, together with the Post Office site, has become a public car park. Fishwick services had operated from the Fox Street bus station since it was opened in the mid/late 1920's, although the 109 Chorley service ran through to Tithebarn Street station via Fox Street in each direction. Prior to using the Fox street station all services ran from roadside bus stops in nearby Corporation Street.

The Fowler bodyshop had meanwhile been busy designing and building its first full size vehicle, which because it was a prototype, had taken twelve months, from the chassis being supplied, a Leyland Tiger Cub PSUC1/12, to complete vehicle delivery in 1970. It had a few unique features: the chassis was the last Tiger Cub to be built, and the completed vehicle was the first to have been produced completely within the Leyland town boundaries since 1954 when Leyland stopped building bus bodies. It is now another privately owned vehicle, preserved in full Fishwick livery.

One of the two Leyland PSU4's with Plaxton Elite bodywork, C5 – VTC716H, seen outside the coach garage Chapel Brow.

Also during that year, five more Leyland Leopard PSU4's arrived. The first two for the coach fleet and had Plaxton Panorama Elite 41-seat bodies. After Fishwicks, one became the PNE Team coach for a period and the other was eventually converted to a recovery vehicle. The remaining three emerged from the Fowler body shop as single deck buses. They incorporated yet another slight change to the livery layout, the introduction of a dark green band around the lower skirt panels in addition to the band around the windows.

1972/3 saw the arrival of three more Leyland Leopards, this time the PSU3 model with Plaxton Panorama Elite 49-seat bodies.

Also in 1972, the first and what proved to be only double deck bus bodied by Fowler emerged from the bodyshop. It was a Leyland Atlantean PDR1/3 having been in storage since built in 1969. The performance was very poor, as the unladen weight, of almost ten tons, proved to be too heavy for the 9.8 litre, (600) engine thus the vehicle only operated for six years. Later that year another Leyland Atlantean arrived, this one was a AN68/1R - to bus grant specification, with an East Lancashire Coachbuilders highbridge body.

Excursions in that year were advertised as follows: -

	adult	child
Blackpool	35p	21p
Morecambe	40p	24p

In 1973 vehicle mileage was around 850,000 carrying 4,000,000 passengers on stage carriage, excursions and private hires.

Over 1973/4, five more buses were completed by the body shop. They were on Daimler Fleetline SRL6-36 chassis with 48-seat single deck 36ft long body configuration; (they were the only single decks Fleetlines that had Leyland engines). These proved to be last 'in house' bus bodies built for the Fishwick fleet influenced by the rising cost of materials and mainly due to the introduction of the integral structured Leyland National. Fowlers bodied eleven Fishwick vehicles altogether. The body shop continued as part of the company until closure in the mid eighties, mainly undertaking major body overhauls, repaints and building car type trailers, which Fishwicks later ran as a trailer hire business.

Mid 1974, two more Leyland Atlantean AN68's with East Lancs highbridge bodies arrived. Both vehicles passed into private ownership and are preserved in full Fishwick livery.

Licences for all stage carriage routes were held jointly with Ribble, although on most of the ten routes operated, Fishwicks dominated almost to the exclusion of Ribble. Also practically all the works services from the Leyland assembly plants were registered as stage carriage services rather than contract work. Contracts however were operated from other factories and schools around the area. By this time about half the services were one man operation. During the week the first bus leaves the depot at 05.00 for works services followed by school runs until 09.00. The afternoon peak time started around 15.00 through to 19.00.

The first examples of the Leyland National single deck bus for Fishwicks arrived in late 1974 and early 1975, and were the first delivered to an independent operator. They were of the 11351/1R type, being 11.3 metres long with single door-layout, 49-seats, and roof mounted heating system. A third example arrived in September 1975 in all-over white as an agreement had been reached with Leyland for the bus to be used as a demonstrator. This was followed at the end of the year by a fourth example of this type. The cost of these vehicles at this time was £21,000.

The first Leyland National Mk1, to be used as a Demonstrator, prior to entering service with the company, was No 15 - NRN838P

In November 1975, two second hand Leyland Leopard coaches with Plaxton Panorama Elite bodywork were acquired, originally new to Wallace Arnold of Leeds. They were only kept for a little over two years, passing to Lancaster Corporation as part of an exchange deal for three short Leyland Nationals.

One of the two Leyland Leopard PSU3's with Plaxton Elite bodywork, new to Wallace Arnold, VUB398H became C1

changeover to one-man-operation in the Fishwicks fleet was also completed during that year. At the end of the year the first Mk 2 Leyland National built to the 'A' series specification arrived, it was also the first Mk 2 to be delivered to an independent operator. As it entered service in early 1980, a sister vehicle arrived in all-over white demonstration livery to replace the previous Mk1 vehicle. Also around this period another new coach arrived a Leopard PSU5D/5R with Duple Dominant II bodywork having 57-seats.

A fourth Leyland Atlantean AN68 with 75-seat East Lanes bodywork arrived in June 1976 which received a slightly revised livery in November 1985.

1977 saw the arrival of seven vehicles, three Nationals at the beginning and two at the end, with two Leopard / Plaxton Supreme coaches mid year. One of each delivery of the Nationals, in turn was again used for demonstration duties. One of the early delivered Nationals, Number 24, which was also initially used for demonstration duties, is another vehicle which passed into private ownership and preservation in May 1997. The two Leopard coaches were delivered in a new livery, which was basically white but included the two shades of green, as used on the service buses. The front panel, just below the windscreen, carried a large gold ' JFS' scroll, with the fleetnames at the same level on the sides above the front wheels. They received a revised livery in early 1984. Another example of this model arrived the following March 1978. Three more Nationals arrived in late 1978, one delivered in all-over white livery taking over demonstration duties.

At the beginning of 1979 another Leopard PSU3E/4R with 53-seat Plaxton Supreme IV Express bodywork arrived. The vehicle passed through a dealer to Pennine, Gargrave, where it operated as a coach until December 1995 and was then converted into a recovery vehicle. The gradual

March of that year saw the first of three ex-prototype / demonstration Leyland Titan B15's, (B15-02), entered service on long-term loan. The second, (B15-04), arrived in September after being initially operated by London Transport. The third (B15-05), arrived in late 1982, when all three were acquired by Fishwicks. Two of these vehicles eventually passed into preservation, one seems to have disappeared but the other has joined several other ex Fishwick vehicles in preservation in a private collection.

Over the next couple of months five more vehicles arrived for the bus fleet. They were three more Mk 2 Nationals and two more unusual /unique vehicles, a Mk 1 10.9-metre Leyland National, originally built in 1973 as a demonstrator for Australia, acquired second hand from Rennies, Dunfermline.

January 1981 saw the arrival of the 23rd Leyland Leopard. It was another PSU5D/5R again with 57- seat Duple Dominant II bodywork. Its delivery brought the coach fleet strength again up to eleven vehicles. C11 - GCK431W.

Chapter One - JOHN FISHWICK & SONS 1907 - 2007

The next vehicle to receive No 23 was GRN895W a Leyland AN69 with ECW bodywork seen after repaint prior to returning to Leyland. Note the adjacent coach, also an ex Fishwick vehicle – EOS formally LIJFS.

The second was a prototype Atlantean AN69A/1R - B20, (Quiet Fleetline), with a 73-seat ECW highbridge body. The vehicle was re-engined c1997 with a 680 engine from one of the East Lancs bodied AN68's.

Two more Mk 2 Leyland National NL116ALll/lR's arrived in December 1981, one again being used for demonstration duties

1982 saw the company become a Public Limited Company.

The first Leyland Tiger arrived for the coach fleet in June 1982, it had a high floor Plaxton Viewmaster 51-seat body. At the end of the year another 11.6-metre Mk 2 Leyland National arrived the first to have a TL11 engine and fully automatic transmission and was used as necessary for demonstration duties. Altogether eight Nationals were loaned back to Leyland for demonstration duties, four Mk1's and four Mk2's. They had Fishwicks legal lettering and fleet numbers from the start in order to comply with bus grant requirements.

The following year, 1983, two new vehicles arrived, the first was another Tiger with the recently introduced Plaxton Paramount 3500 body with a cherished registration number, LSB 83, the letters being the initials of the

daughter of one of the Directors. The second vehicle was a 33 foot Leyland Atlantean AN69, which had been built in 1978 as a left hand drive version of the B20 for Baghdad. The chassis was purchased in May 1981, converted to right hand drive and sent to Eastern Coach Works in Lowestoft for bodying with an Olympian style highbridge single door body. It entered service early in the New Year. The mid 1980's, saw the closure and sale of the Fowler premises in Hastings Road. The repair work was transferred to the Golden Hill garage, where it is still undertaken.

1985/6 saw mainly new vehicle arrivals for the coach fleet. The first five all had Plaxton Paramount 3500 bodies, two Tigers (one of which had another cherished registration number, VKY 43) and three DAF MB200's was a departure from the long standing 'policy' of operating Leyland Group vehicles. Two others were Leyland Royal Tiger integrals with the Workington built Doyen bodywork. Towards the end of 1986 two of the new National replacement single deck buses arrived which were Leyland Lynx. They were followed by two more in June 1987. Also that year the coach-leasing programme continued with the arrival of five more DAF's, two SB230's and three MB230's all having Van Hool Alizee bodywork.

One of two Leyland Royal Tiger Doyens C753MFR – C12

D619YCX - C16 was a DAF SB230 with Van Hool bodywork operating throughout the lease period in a silver livery except with the addition of fleet names. Seen here in Keswick coach park.

As a result of deregulation, introduced on 26 October 1986, the joint working agreement with Ribble terminated. Fishwicks registered five services, they had previously been operating, which were:-

109   PRESTON - CHORLEY via Leyland and Euxton.
111   LEYLAND - PRESTON via Lostock Hall.
115   LEYLAND - PRESTON
       via Farrinton Moss, Whitestake and Penwortham.
       (Re-routing of old Seven Stars
       via Croston Road service)
117   LEYLAND - PRESTON via Bamber Bridge.
       Since re-routed to include Walton Summit.
119   LEYLAND - CHORLEY
       detour of 109 to include Runshaw College.

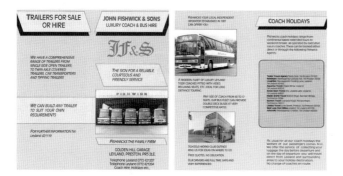

The most intense of these services was/is the 111 route which operates from 06.00 with last return from Preston at 23.20. During the week, daytime operating has a 15-minute headway reducing to 40-minute in the evening. The Saturday running has a 20-minute

headway during the day reducing to 40-minute in the evening and hourly throughout Sunday. They also decided to operate a mini bus service around the housing estates of Leyland, responding to local needs and stave off the opposition which was threatening the area. Four second-hand, Freight Rover Sherpas with Optare, 16 coach seated bodies initially began the service. The livery on these vehicles was similar to that on the standard stage carriage vehicles, i.e. two tone green, but were given a variation to the fleetname -

'FishKwick', and a new fleet numbering series with prefix 'M'. Due to the popularity

FishKwick Emblem

of these services a demonstration vehicle was loaned from Reeve-Burgess, which had an Iveco chassis, whilst new vehicles could be sourced.

Also around this time another threat came on the main 111 route by another local operator, Mercers of Longridge but it was only for short period as their routes were taken over by Ribble.

A review of the fleet after eighty years, in mid 1987, comprised a total of 45 vehicles, as follows:

21 single deck buses	11 x Leyland National Mk 1
	8 x Leyland National Mk 2
	4 x Leyland Lynx Mk 1
5 double deck buses	3 x Leyland Atlantean AN68
	2 x Leyland Atlantean AN69
4 mini buses	4 x Freight Rover Sherpa
15 coaches	4 x Leyland Leopard
	4 x Leyland Tiger
	2 x Leyland Royal Tiger
	2 x DAF SB230
	3 x DAF MB230

Five more mini buses joined the fleet in the latter part of 1987, which had Mercedes Benz 609D/709D chassis's with Reeve Burgess bodies. The livery favoured the coach livery, i.e. mainly white with the two tone green bands. Also around this time another Freight Rover based vehicle was used on short-term loan.

The early part of 1988 saw many changes to the coach fleet with six new DAF/Van Hool's replacing five of the same type and four new Leyland Tigers/Plaxton

Paramount's replacing the two Royal Tigers. This brought the coach fleet strength for the 1988 season to eighteen. Also that year, the tenth mini bus entered service, which was another Mercedes Benz 609D again with Reeve Burgess bodywork. The total operating fleet at this time had risen to 56 vehicles.

During the summer coaching season, one of the Tigers failed at the Watford Gap Services on the M1 motorway. The Scammell recovery vehicle was despatched to bring it home, but as the Scammell approached Charnock Richard on the M6 motorway with the Tiger on tow, it decided to give up the ghost. Fortunately, it was close enough to base for both vehicles to be easily retrieved. The Scammell was, soon after, replaced by an Atkinson Borderer with a 14-litre Cummins engine. This was registered Q27 GHG, as trade plates could no longer be used on recovery vehicles.

The following year 1989 saw an intake of six new coaches and two more Reeve Burgess bodied Mercedes Benz 609D's mini buses with coach seats replacing the Sherpa vehicles. The coaches were four Tigers with Plaxton Paramount 3500 Mk V bodies and two Bova Futuras, which were a totally new concept of vehicle for the company. A new style livery was tried on one of the Bova's, which included curved stripes of green on a white background. Two of the AN68 Atlanteans were placed in store along side number 23 stored the previous year all returning to service in September 1990 as new school contracts had been acquired. During summer 1989 a demonstrator DAF Optare single deck bus was inspected and used over the various routes for evaluation although none were ordered.

During the early part of 1990, there was a strong rumour that the bus side of the business was to be taken over by Stagecoach, which had already made inroads into other local bus operations such as Ribble and Cumberland. Fortunately, the rumour was without any foundation and the

Another ex Demonstration vehicle was D84BLF a Mercedes 709D with coach seated Reeves Burgess bodywork seen prior to receiving the FishKwick livery and fleet No M8.

agreement made some years previously, with Ribble, continued with Stagecoach.

1990 saw the delivery of four coach replacements, Tiger/ Plaxtons being returned and two further similar vehicles along with two Volvo B10 M / Van Hool Alizee which was another different type of vehicle for the fleet.

The next vehicles to arrive were for the stage carriage fleet and were two Mk 2 Leyland Lynx's in March 1991.

Also around this time two further coaches arrived which had been new Parks of Hamilton and were Volvo's with Plaxton bodies. They remained in the delivered livery of white and orange but had fleet names along the side and the 'JFS' scroll to the front upper windscreens. With the coaches frequently changing, the

A view of the Chapel Brow coach garage with four Leyland Tiger / Plaxton Paramount coaches and one of the two Bova's parked ready for the next day's work.

The second vehicle to receive an all – over advertisement was No5 Leyland Lynx 2, H65CCK.

fleet number system for coaches was terminated, and duty allocation was by the registration number. One of the tours operated that year was a first for the company and was a 5000 mile journey to the Arctic Circle, were the passengers experienced 24 hours of daylight creating a false sense of time. Also during 1991 six new coaches arrived, two DAF's with Van Hool Alizee bodies, one carrying another special registration number J9 JFS and four more ex Parks Volvo BlOM's with Plaxton Paramount bodies which received full Fishwicks green and white coach livery. Over the previous nine years a total of twenty-two Plaxton Paramount 's were operated by the company, thirteen with Leyland Tiger chassis, three DAF and six Volvo B10M chassis. A third Mk 2 Leyland Lynx arrived towards the end of the year followed by a fourth one in March 1992. Both had special registration numbers J7 JFS and J14 JFS.

Three vehicles came for the 1992 holiday season, two Volvo BlOM's with the new Plaxton Premiere bodywork, which received special registration numbers K3 JFS and K4 JFS. The third was a Mercedes Benz 814D with Autobus Classique 29- seat bodywork, shortly after delivery was re-registered K5 JFS. It was initially used on a special contract for British Gas, North West, but was later used on private hire and excursion work.

During 1993, two single deck demonstrator buses were evaluated. The first was a 'J' registered Dennis Lance with Plaxton Pointer bodywork, the second was a 'K' registered DAF with Ikarus bodywork. Following evaluation periods of one to two weeks, no orders were placed. Towards the end of that year more Mk 1

Nationals were either placed in store at Chapel Brow or sold. Also around this time, more school contracts were won which required more double deck vehicles. To cover the requirement two ex Thamesdown Leyland Fleetiine FE30AGR with ECW bodywork were purchased, which were new in 1978. They operated for four years and then passed to a local film company.

A further change in vehicle leasing came the following year with the arrival of an EOS 90. It remained in an all-silver livery, although standard fleet names and dark green bands were added and carried special registration LI JFS. Another coach arrived the following month, which was another DAF SB3000 with Van Hool Alizee bodywork. It was on a short-term lease being returned to the dealer within six months.

Two single deck demonstrator buses were evaluated during the early - mid part of 1994. The first was a Volvo B10B with Alexander bodywork, and the other a Marshall-bodied Dennis Dart. No orders were placed: instead, it was decided to have two of the Mk 1 Nationals, re-engined with DAF engines, along with modifications to the heating and ventilation systems. The work was carried out by Hughes DAF followed by two more the following year. August 1994 saw the arrival of two more second-hand double deck vehicles, Bristol VRT/SL3/6LXB's with 74-seat ECW bodywork, new originally to Keighley and District in 1978 and 1980. The policy of purchasing second hand Double deck vehicles rather than new ones was adopted as Lancashire County Council school/ college contracts were short term and could not be guaranteed on a long term basis. Another first for Fishwicks came in September when one of the Mk 2 Nationals, number 26, received an all-over advertising livery for Foley's Insurance of Leyland returning to fleet livery in October 1996. Over 1994 operating mileage on stage carriage work exceeded 1,500,000, and around 1,200,000 on coach operation with eighty employees.

May 1995 two further Mk 1 Nationals were placed in store at Chapel Brow, one of which, number 24 passed into preservation in December 1999. Also during 1995 many changes to the coach fleet with two more EOS 90's, one receiving special registration J9 JFS from a previous vehicle, both in a new livery, mainly white with green stripes and gold artwork depicting the company's choice in world-wide holiday tours. Another DAF/ Van Hool, taking the special registration number K3 JFS followed them in March. Shortly after entering service it was given Leger Holidays livery, but still carried FISHWICK fleetnames along the sides and at the front and rear. The next month two Volvo BlOM's with Plaxton Excalibur bodies arrived in fleet livery.

The four Wright bodied Dennis Dart's photographed on arrival ironically adjacent to the entrance of Leyland Spurrier works. R845-8VEC - No's 15, 17-19

J. FISHWICK & SONS ROUTES

Route Map circa mid 1995

In 1996, after initially being used by the dealer for shows and demonstration work, a fourth EOS 90, with a slightly different version of the livery was added. This was followed a few months later by another DAF/Van Hool, which replaced the previous vehicle of this type on Leger work. With an increase in work on the stage carriage side of the business, around autumn, two DAF SB220 single-deck buses with Northern Counties bodywork were leased short term, thus only receiving fleet names on the all-over white livery. They returned to the dealers the following April.

New coach deliveries in 1997 again favoured the DAF/Van Hool combination, both joining the previous one, being used mainly on Leger work. The last vehicles to join the fleet up to 90 years, saw another change to previous policy being the first new non Leyland stage carriage vehicles. They were four Dennis Dart SLF single deck low floor buses with Wright Crusader bodies. The company at this time employed around 70, of which there were 34 stage carriage drivers and 13 coach drivers.

The fleet, in September 1997, after 90 years, comprised of 45 vehicles, which were as follows:

25 single deck buses	5 x Leyland National Mk 1
	8 x Leyland National Mk 2
	4 x Leyland Lynx Mk 1
	4 x Leyland Lynx Mk 2
	4 x Dennis Dart SLF
5 double deck buses	1 x Leyland Atlantean AN68
	2 x Leyland Atlantean AN69
	2 x Bristol VRT
7 mini buses	6 x Mercedes Benz 609D
	1 x Mercedes Benz 709D
8 coaches	3 x EOS 90
	2 x Volvo B10M
	3 x DAF SB3000

To commemorate the 90 years operation a special event was staged in September, the four Dennis Dart's receiving a 90 years logo on the front panels. Several old and new vehicles attended the event particularly from operators, which the company had been associated with over the years.

THE FOLLOWING CORRECTIONS HAVE BEEN IDENTIFIED
SINCE RELEASE OF THE FIRST PUBLICATION - John Fishwick & Sons   1907 - 1997

Original Page Numbers	Page Reference	Fleet	Registration	Original Text Numbers	Corrected Text
6-29	Text			General	See Pages 6-23/5/6
23	Text RHS			...The trials never commenced. ...converted to single door 1919...	It was a trial for about 2 years. Conversion carried out previously by Merseyside. 1914...
33	Lower Photo text			1919	1914 .....
42	Centre Photo text			... duties in 1979	... 1968
75	Top Right Photo text			Ex-number 4 ...	14 .....
81	Top Photo Text			..seen back in Leyland	..seen Albert Dock Liverpool
82-88	Fleet List			General	See Page 79-86
82	Fleet List	22	TE1014	Chassis Type SWQ Chassis Number 215912	See Page 79
		13	TE7864	Chassis Number 60416 Notes 1. H 1/ 52	See Page 79
		16	TE7862	Chassis Number 60414 Notes 1. H 4/ 52	See Page 79
83	Fleet List	1	TF5919	Chassis Number 72121 Notes 1. H 5/ 53	See Page 79
		2	TF5920	Chassis Number 72122 Notes 1. H 1/ 56	See Page 79
		3	TF5921	Chassis Number 72120	See Page 79
		7	GTD598	Chassis Type PS1/1	See Page 80
		11	GTE395	Chassis Type PS1/1	See Page 80
		8	HTE954	Chassis Type PS1/1	See Page 80
		15	HTE955	Chassis Type PS1/1	See Page 80
		34	KTJ481	Chassis Number 493300	See Page 80
		24	KTJ482	Chassis Number 493299	See Page 80
		16	NTC233	Chassis Type HR40	See Page 80
		17	NTC234	Chassis Type HR40	See Page 80
84	Fleet List	11	523CTF	Seating Capacity B44 F	See Page 80
		15	525CTF	Body Number LW50	See Page 80
		28	524CTF	Seating Capacity B44 F Body Number LW51	See Page 80
85	Fleet List	27	BTD780J	Chassis Number 903108	See Page 81
		16	BTD779J	Chassis Number 903109	See Page 81
		C5	BTB779L		See Page 81
		5	PTC124M	Chassis Number 00923	See Page 82
		3	PTC123M	Chassis Number 00924	See Page 82
		14	PCK193P	Chassis Number 02819	See Page 82
86	Fleet List	13	TLS733P	Seating Capacity B49 F	See Page 82
88	Fleet List		M664WCK	Chassis Number 042631 Body Number ...2998	See Page 85
			M665WCK	Chassis Number 042630 Body Number ...2993	See Page 85
90	Fleet Summary		J976KHD		See Page 88
91	Re Registrations		FSU392		See Page 89
92	Breakdown and Service Vehicles	Atkinson Borderer	Q827GHG		Q27GHG

ITEMS UNDERLINED WERE INCORRECT IN ORIGINAL PUBLICATION CORRECTIONS SEE RELEVENT REFERENCE PAGE

Chapter Two
The Family

John Fishwick was born in 1862. Early in the 20th century he decided to move from Wales, to the Lancashire area to work. I have been informed, on numerous occasions, by my mother that he worked with my grandfather at, what was originally, the Lancashire Steam Motor Company. In 1907, frustrated by long period of unemployment, he purchased a Steam Wagon and start his own company.

View of the house (LHS), from Golden Hill Lane, where John Fishwick and his family lived up to 1947. Taken c1950

The business prospered and moved from haulage to include passenger services, stage carriage, coach hire, holidays, mini bus services, bus body construction and trailer hire.

John lived at 124 Golden Hill Lane (known as Richmond House Farm), and acquired the land behind to build, what is still the current garages. The house was also used as the office and later, in 1947, passed to an employee.

In early 1967, Richmond House Farm was demolished to build a new workshop and extend the garage, however the Council objected and the current staff restroom / canteen was erected instead.

John Fishwick was a member of the Leyland Golf Club and became the club's first Captain in

1924/5. His generosity over the years provided the club with its first club house, a former bus body from one of the early vehicles.

John Fishwick had four sons William, Bernard, Vincent and James (Jack).

At the outbreak of World War I, help was on hand when William and Bernard started as drivers. Bernard also acted as conductor for the weekend journeys and he continued up to the early thirties.

When John Fishwick retired, his sons William, Bernard, Vincent and James (Jack) set up a partnership. John, however, continued to take an interest in the business and was actively involved in the day to day operations.

John Fishwick died in 1934 at the age of 63. On the day of his funeral, one of the drivers detoured from his service route past the cemetery to salute the funeral cortege as it arrived then continued on his scheduled service.

After their fathers death, William was duly appointed General Manager / Chief Engineer and Bernard Company Secretary.

William was born in Wales and moved with the family to Euxton where he went to school. In 1914 he became an apprentice fitter at the Chorley factory of Leyland Motors and in his spare time was an unpaid

View from the back yard of 124 Golden Hill Lane, looking into vehicle yard

JOHN FISHWICK & SONS 1907 - 2007 - Chapter Two

conductor. By the mid 1940's William assumed responsibility for running the company.

A former President of the Leyland Cricket and Bowling Club, William was also a keen walker and cyclist. He was also instrumental in the construction of the Shaw Hill Golf club.

William never retired from the firm continuing as a partner until his death, at 79 on Christmas Eve 1977.

James was unfortunately killed in a flying accident in World War II.

Bernard and Vincent have also died.

William's grandson (John Fishwick's great grandson) John C. Brindle joined the company in 1962, straight from school. He did everything in his first year from washing vehicles to conducting and inspecting. John is now Managing Director / General Manager and occasionally, when drivers are at a premium, he takes to the wheel.

William Fishwick one of John Fishwicks sons

In June 2003 John Brindle received an MBE for his services to the bus industry. He has two daughters, Laura and Victoria born 1975 and 1976 respectively.

Bernard's grandsons James F. Hustler and Miles Cassum joined the company in 1973 and 1982.

James took his grandfather's position as Company Secretary and Director and is also seen out driving on school or service runs as the need arises. He is the proud father of Isobele born 2004 and Thomas born 2006

John Fishwick with his Leyland X2 and bus body conversion

Towards the end of the month prior to the 90 year celebratory event in August, two more Bristol VRT/ ECW's arrived for school contract work. They were originally new to West Yorkshire Road Car in 1978 and 1980 and had similar specifications to the previous two. In October, DAF SB3000/ Van Hool, K3JFS was returned to the dealers, at the end of the coaching season, Fishwicks retaining the registration. It then passed to Moxhams, Worksop then Lutterworth Coaches, Lutterworth.

February 1998 another coach, the M reg. EOS, was also returned to the dealers in preparation for the new coaches arriving in April. These were two DAF SB 3000's with the newly introduced Van Hool T9 body. Both were initially used for Fishwicks own tour work but one was latterly used for Leger tours receiving this livery after repaint following an accident. At this time a second EOS, J9JFS, was also returned to the dealers, registration again being retained by the company. The first EOS returned now operates with Leander, Swadlingcote and the second with Ogdens, St. Helens.

The following year, 1999, began again with only changes in the coach fleet. In April the ' N ' registered EOS was exchanged for another DAF SB 3000/ Van Hool T9. Then the following month another exchange was made by replacing the 'N' registration DAF SB 3000/ Van Hool Alizee T8 with a 'T' reg. of the same type for the Leger tour work.

*John Fishwick & Sons 90th Anniversary Event,
pictured above left Event Leaflet, above right Event Programme*

To celebrate 90 years an open day took place on Sunday 28th September 1997 at the two Fishwicks premises, Tuer street and Chapel Brow and also at the British Commercial Vehicle Museum in King Street. The three sites were linked with a bus service, operated by Fishwicks and other visiting vintage vehicles, many from local operators with previous associations to the company. The main Leyland to Preston route 111 saw a more intense frequency for a Sunday with both Fishwick and vintage vehicles being operated to cater for the expected number of visitors and enthusiasts wishing to travel with a special Day Rover Ticket.

*The fourth DAF SB3000 / Van Hool Alizee used on Leger work was
T57AUA.*

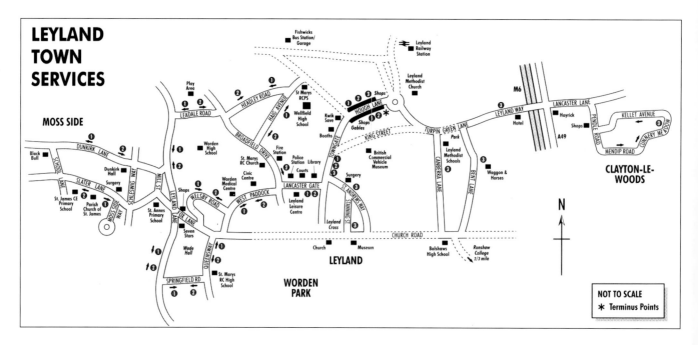

LEYLAND TOWN SERVICES

MOSS SIDE

CLAYTON-LE-WOODS

LEYLAND

WORDEN PARK

N

NOT TO SCALE
* Terminus Points

Leyland Town Services from 27th September 1997 wer as follows:

Route 1	Leyland Hough Lane Roundabout
	Broadfield Estate
	Moss Side
	Springfield Estate
	Civic Centre
	Hough Lane Roundabout.
Route 2	Leyland Hough Lane Roundabout
	Civic Centre
	Springfield Estate
	Moss Side
	Broadfield Estate
	Hough Lane Roundabout.
Route 3	Clayton-le-Woods
	Stoney Lane
	Hayrick
	Hough Lane
	Leyland Cross

Towards the end of the year, in October, two more Bristol VRT/ ECW were purchased for school contract work. These originated from Southdown, new in 1980 and Devon General new in 1981.

On Monday 15th November a revision to the timetable of the 116 "express" service (Moss Side to Preston) was introduced. A further revision came in 2006 when the afternoon and Saturday services ceased. The following month another single deck demonstration vehicle was evaluated, which was a Volvo B6 with a Wright Crusader body.

Rail Excursion Brochure

Two notable events, which occurred during that year, were firstly, the opportunity of Rail excursions were added to the excursion program.

Secondly the bus wars, which previously occurred in the early 20th century, reoccurring briefly after de-regulation, raised its head again on the main Leyland to Preston route 111. Blue Bus from

One of the latest two EOS 90's and another design of livery - Y477HUA

Chapter Three - JOHN FISHWICK & SONS 1907 - 2007

The last mini bus to join the fleet was a Mercedes T814 with an Alexander body. Fleet No 29 – T154AUA.

dealers. This vehicle eventually joined the 'N' reg. of the same type at Jones, Flint North Wales. A month earlier, April saw the exchange of the two ' M ' registered Volvo / Plaxton Excalibur for two more EOS's for Fishwicks tours. Both passed to Zak's, Birmingham, then Premiere, Nottingham with one passing to Dixon t/a Rainbow Billingham, joining one of the 'G' reg. Volvo B10M / Plaxtons.

Towards the end of the year, September / October due to some main route alterations duplicating Mini Bus routes, the later were withdrawn resulting in three of the Mini Buses being withdrawn and sold. The second of the 'P' registered DAF/ Van Hool Leger coaches was returned to the dealers during October.

near by Horwich, decided to operate on the main route operated by Fishwicks, which subsidized some of the other routes operated by them. The opposing company, however, only operated during the peak period weekdays and on Saturdays. To combat this position, Fishwicks had to reduce frequencies of the 117 Bamber Bridge service. This enabled them to operate a ten-minute frequency, which together with the early morning evening and Sunday services continuing running, eventually secured the service being mainly operated by them. It was 2001 that Blue Bus cut back to operating a much reduced frequency with an extended route 113 to/from Wigan. They eventually terminated the whole service through Leyland in 2005 and were eventually taken over by Arriva

The turn of the century into 2000 saw many changes in all sections to the whole fleet. In February another DAF SB220 / Northern Counties single deck bus arrived in all white on short-term loan. This loan was due to the delay of a new vehicle delivery. This vehicle was the first example of a new model, which had been exhibited at the previous motor show then returned to the manufacturers for modifications prior to release to Fishwicks. It was a DAF SB 120 with a Wright Cadet body and received the special registration, which had previously been used on an EOS - L1JFS. Also during May one of the ' P ' registered DAF/ Van Hool Leger coaches was returned to the

Also between October and December the six Bristol VRT's were replaced, three passed to Alphine, Llandudno, one to an operator in the north of Scotland and the other two scrapped by Fishwicks. The replacement vehicles arriving November to January 01 were five former Preston Transport Alexander bodied Leyland Atlantean's painted in Fishwicks livery prior to arrival.

Two more DAF SB 220's were loaned in November, one was similar to the previous short term loan vehicles having Northern Counties bodywork and the second having Northern Counties / Plaxton bodywork. This

Rear offside view of No40, the new DAF SB200 with Wright Commander body

Front nearside view of No39 opposite the old Leyland Police station, the new DAF SB200 with Wright Commander body

vehicle was initially christened the 'Barbie Bus' as it had a pink roof and pink interior and was built in 1999.

During January and February 2001, two loan vehicles were returned to the dealers, firstly one of the ' R ' registered DAF / Van Hool T9's, followed by the DAF SB 220 / NC single deck bus. The other SB 220, known as the 'Barbie Bus' was taken into stock and painted into full Fishwick livery. Also during February three more DAF SB 120's with similar bodies to the earlier prototype i.e. Wright Cadet entered service.

These were followed, late March - early April, by two more EOS coaches one each for Fishwick and Leger tours. The former one was also later used on Leger work.

Mid year, August saw the arrival of another unique vehicle to the fleet in the form of a Mercedes Benz T814 with 27 seat Alexander bodywork. It was originally built in 1999 and acquired to supplement the Mini bus workings and any private hire requirements.

During September three more Mini buses were withdrawn from service and sold, an 'E' and two 'F' registered ones. New operators of these vehicles were scattered throughout the country, Yorkshire, Hampshire, Northumberland and Warrington. This meant that only one of the original Mini's and the newly

acquired vehicle remained as a result of the Mini bus services being replaced.

The following month, October, the other 'R' registered DAF / VH T9 was returned to the dealers at the end of the Leger tour season.

Into February 2002 before the next change to the fleet occurred and was to be the last new EOS to be operated by Fishwicks, although three other, 'T, W and R' registered examples were operated on one to two month short term loan periods over the next eighteen months. This was due to the take over of EOS by Van Hool and rationalization of models.

On the bus side DAF had introduced a new model, SB 200, which had a 6-cylinder engine, Fishwicks decided to have one on trial for a month for evaluation.

YJ03PDU a DAF SB4000 / Van Hool Alizee T9, one of the first to receive the 'Classic Gold Holidays' Livery.

As a result two vehicles of this type with Wright Commander arrived in August.

Vehicles returned at the end of the tour season were the two 'T' registration DAF / Van Hool's. The T8 version eventually joined a previously returned example of the same type at Geldards, Leeds and the T9 version operated with the two 'R' reg. T9's at Selwyns, Runcorn on initially on National Express work.

The replacement coaches arrived in February 2003 entering service at the beginning of April and were to

Fleet No 42 – YJ03PFF

the new DAF SB 4000 specification with Van Hool T9 bodies with reduced seating to 42 for the newly released Classic Gold Tours program. The livery had changed on each previous delivery over the last few years, however the one adapted on these two continued over the next few years. It began with white at the front blending mid way into light green then into dark green at the rear. Very large gold 'JF & S' schrolls appeared about the rear wheels and on the rear of the vehicle. John Fishwick & Sons was in gold over each of the front wheels with Classic Gold Holidays following in white.

Also in March came two more DAF SB 200 / Wright Commander single deck buses similar specification to the previous ones.

These new vehicles resulted in a hastily disposal of the last four Mk 1 Leyland National's, which had been kept in service due to the re-engine/ refurbishment undertaken in 1995, the vehicles having been new in 1977/8 i.e. 25 years service. Two were converted to mobil classrooms for a Milk supply company, one converted to a mobil hospitality unit for a Church group and the other eventually scrapped due to gearbox problems.

In July another vehicle was sold, it was the last of the four Leyland AN68's with East Lancs bodies, which had been in store since March 2001, and was converted to a mobile music center in the South Cumbria area.

The first Mk2 Leyland National to be withdrawn in November, was number 10, which was also the first National 2 demonstrator. It was initially placed in store, at Chapel Brow, parts being removed when required for other vehicles, including the engine for number 12. The remains were eventually taken to the Ribble

Preservation Group for salvage of panels and other body parts (for possible use on the Ribble National restoration) and base shell eventually scrapped in January 2005. Also that month one of the 'W' registered EOS coaches was returned to the dealers, later being acquired by Quantock MS, Somerset then Butler, Kirby in Ashfield.

Late January / early February 2004 saw the arrival of two more DAF SB200's again with Wright Commander bodies similar to the previous deliveries. They replaced the first of the Leyland Mk1 Lynx's to be withdrawn after engine failure, which after rectification by the new owner was sold on into Southern Ireland.

More new vehicles arrived in March for the coach fleet, they were DAF SB4000's again with Van Hool T9 bodies. One was to the 'Classic Gold Holiday' specification and the other two were for Leger work but to their 'Silver Service' specification. All entered service in April when the two 'Y' registered EOS's were returned to the dealers. Over the next few years of operation the new Leger coaches were hardly ever seen at base, travelling to destinations as far as Russia.

With the local college being just on the outskirts of town, an opportunity was seen to operate a more frequent short working of the 109 route which passes Runshaw College, branded service 999, with a fixed flat fare of 30p. Initially one of the remaining Mk11 Nationals is used estimated loading being around 500/day.

Later in September/early October saw the arrival three more second hand vehicles for the stage carriage fleet, this time from Lothian (Edinburgh). They were Leyland Olympian's with Alexander two door bodies. Prior to the last one entering service a conversion to single door was undertaken and the other two converted soon after. These vehicles were mainly used on the main stage carriage route, 111 Leyland to Preston immediately as they entered service with Fishwicks.

The first of the ex Preston Alexander bodied Leyland Atlanteans was withdrawn, after engine failure (engines and parts becoming more difficult to obtain) and after a few months in store, parts being removed to keep other

Leyland Olympian with Alexander bodywork No34 – F355WSC, one of three acquired from Lothian Transport, seen prior to conversion to single door.

vehicles of this type on the road, was eventually scrapped in September.

This was followed in November by the other three Mk1 Lynx's being withdrawn and sold almost immediately, all three eventually finding their way across to Southern Ireland, one eventually passing to Kells Bus Museum, Cork. The other 'W' registered EOS was returned to the dealers in November.

The final change came in late December when two more DAF SB120's with Wright Cadet bodies arrived but did not enter service until the New Year. The vehicles only had a four-cylinder engine and reduced seating from 44 (Commander bodied examples) to 39.

March 2005 saw the arrival of a new coach for the Fishwick Classic Gold Tours and was to the same specification as the previous year's deliveries i.e. DAF SB4000/ Van Hool T9 Alizee.

Also during March the Mercedes T814 midi bus was sold, having been in store since the previous December after the Mini bus routes had ceased. It was sold locally to Elite Travel at Carlton, Blackpool.

During June, two of the Mk2 National's, which had been withdrawn earlier in the year when the new vehicles entered service, were taken out of store, one being scrapped and the other moved and

placed in the corner of the yard at Golden Hill to be used as a store shed, both having all serviceable parts previously removed.

Two more vehicles for the stage carriage fleet came in September, which again were DAF SB200's with Wright Commander bodies bringing the total DAF SB's operating with Wright bodies to 14. The two vehicles displaced were another Mk2 National and the first of the Mk2 Lynx's, the later being placed in store and the former parked along side the adapted store at the Golden Hill garage. At the beginning of the following month, October, the last of EOS coaches was returned to the dealers after a three and a half-year lease period. Altogether nine of this type of vehicle, EOS, were leased on long term and a further three on short-term loan.

The first vehicle to leave the fleet in 2006, February, was one of the two DAF SB4000/ Van Hool's operating in the Leger livery. It went directly to Staintons, Kendal, along with the remaining Leger contract.

The first, and only new vehicle to arrive in 2006, was a DAF SB4000 / Van Hool T9 Alizee coach, again similar specification to previous ones i.e. 42 seats. It arrived early March in Fishwicks livery without Classic Gold Tours logo, but only began operating in April.

In 2004 Lancashire County Council pioneered a system in the Preston area known as 'realtime'. It was to

View of modified bus stop incorporating 'Real-time' with information leaflet issued by Lancashire County Council.

Chapter Three - JOHN FISHWICK & SONS 1907 - 2007

Lancashire County Council Realtime leaflet

provide up to the minute information about local bus services giving the time arriving at the particular stop you were waiting at. Besides keeping passengers informed, it also gives buses priority if they are delayed at selected road junctions and traffic lights. 'realtime' was initially introduced on the Preston City centre routes, In all twenty-six bus stops between Preston and Leyland were fitted with electronic displays which inform the passengers of the services and times. The system control / information originates from the TGX ticket machine, which transmits a signal to the bus stops, signals and base using the Global Positioning Satellite (GPS) technology. In addition to on street displays, information is also available on the Internet and mobil phone text messages. The control for the Fishwicks operations are from their main office in Tuer Street, were operations originally began.

With the local college being just on the outskirts of town, an opportunity was seen to operate a more frequent short working of the 109 route which passes Runshaw College, branded service 999, with a fixed flat fare of 30p. Initially one of the remaining Mk11 Nationals is used estimated loading being around 500/day.

Other route changes over the past few years have been to the 109, which again seeing potential from the former Royal Ordinance Factory closer to become a large housing development, Buckshaw Village, re-routing to take in this development. The other was the 115 route (Croston Road) re-routed through Higher Penwortham and extended to Chorley via Euxton (Bay Horse), which means a direct weekday service from Penwortham to Chorley Hospital becoming available.

Late September 2006 two more Leyland / Alexander Olympians again from Lothian Transport, arrived painted in the light green.

They were taken the next day to S&T, part of East Lancashire Coach Builders, to have the centre doors removed. On return the dark green livery and fleet names were added and they entered service at the restart of school term, late October.

The first change to the fleet in 2007 came in early January, when the two 03 reg. DAF SB4000 / Van Hool coaches were returned to Arriva. Also at the beginning of the year each of the service vehicles received a Centenary Emblem in the first nearside bay window. Towards the end of February/beginning of March the last three ex Preston Atlanteans were also taken to the scrap yard.

To celebrate the Centenary year, two DAF SB200's and DAF SB4000 vehicles were delivered. The single deck vehicles had the new Plaxton Centro 45 seat bodies and the coaches Van Hool Alizee T9 bodywork with a similar livery to the previous examples. The two coaches, and one single deck, arrived towards the end of February, the latter, which had previously been exhibited by Plaxton at the November Bus & Coach show in Birmingham, entered service on the 1st March 2007. The second DAF SB200 came in the middle of March and was put into service a couple of days later

Two more ex Lothian Alexander bodied Olympians, on the M6 north of Tebay en route to Leyland. G806/2GSX became No's 31 & 30.

after the Realtime equipment had been installed. The two coaches were kept in store, starting tours at the beginning of April.

Towards the end of March another DAF SB200 with Wright Commander bodywork, arrived on short term loan agreement, as similar vehicle No41 had been involved in a serious accident, which was not the fault of the bus driver, and would be out of duty for around four weeks. The replacement vehicle ran in all white with fleet name and was given temporary number 50 for fuelling purposes.

A further Demonstration vehicle was evaluated in April, a silver painted Mercedes Citaro with seating capacity of 41 plus 28 standees.

The fleet in July 2007, after 100 years, comprised of 43 vehicles which are as follows:

30 single deck buses	5 x Leyland National Mk 2
	4 x Leyland Lynx Mk 2
	4 x Dennis Dart SLF
	6 x DAF SB120
	1 x DAF SB220
	11 x DAF SB200
7 double deck buses	2 x Leyland Atlantean AN69
	5 x Leyland Olympian
6 coaches	6 x DAF SB4000

Sad to see, as with many other former 'all Leyland' operators, only a few of the originally new vehicles remain in the fleet. One thing that has remained throughout the Century of operation is the request from John Fishwick himself that the livery for the buses should continue to be light and dark green.

John Fishwick & Sons   BUS ROUTES 2007

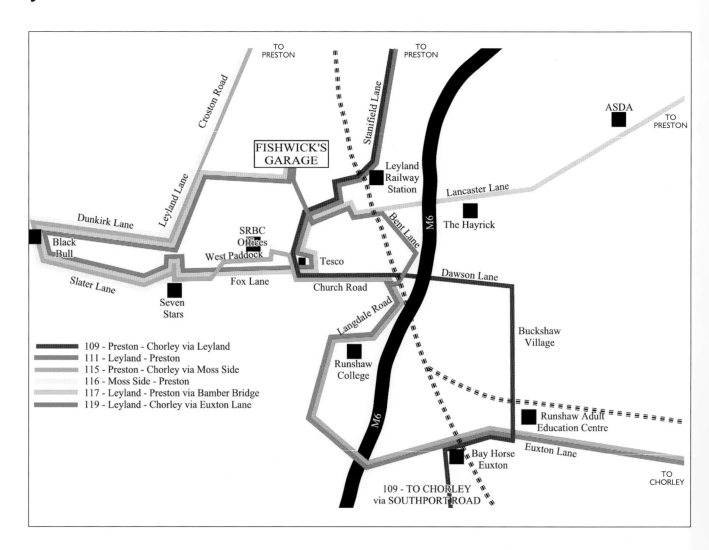

PRESTON - PENWORTHAM - LEYLAND   111
Monday to Friday

					A		A
				NF	F	NF	F	F
PRESTON Bus Station [76]	0625		1815		2245	2245	2315		232
PRESTON Fishergate	0629		1819		2249	2249	2319	2322	2324
PENWORTHAM New Lane	0634	and	1824	and	2254	2254	2324	2327	2329
LOSTOCK HALL Library	0639	every	1829	every	2259	2259	2329	2332	2334
LEYLAND Gables	0648	10	1838	30	2308	2308	2338	2341	2343
LEYLAND Tesco Store	0651	mins	1841	mins	2311	2311	2341	2344	2346
MOSS SIDE Black Bull	0659	until	1849	unti	2319	2319	2349	2352	2354
LEYLAND Fishwicks Garage	0705		1855		2325	2325	2355	2358	2400

NF - Not Fridays   F - Friday Only
A - On Fridays these journeys operate from Preston Bus Stn via Ringway and Lune Street, ommitting the bus stop at Waterstones Book Shop

LEYLAND - PENWORTHAM - PRESTON   111
Monday to Friday

LEYLAND Fishwicks Garage	0600	0605		1630		1730		2230
MOSS SIDE Black Bull		0611		1637		1736		2236
LEYLAND St.Andrews Way (Tesco)		0619	and	1646	and	1744	and	2244
LEYLAND opp The Gables		0622	every	1649	every	1747	every	2247
LEYLAND Station Brow	0602	0624	10	1651	15	1749	30	2249
LOSTOCK HALL Library	0609	0631	mins	1659	mins	1756	mins	2256
PENWORTHAM New Lane	0613	0635	until	1705	until	1800	until	2300
PRESTON Opp Railway Station	0618	0640		1710		1805		2305
PRESTON Bus Station	0623	0645		1715		1810		2310

PRESTON - PENWORTHAM - LEYLAND   111
Saturday

PRESTON Bus Station [76]	0700		2320
PRESTON Fishergate	0704	then	2324
PENWORTHAM New Lane	0709	every	2329
LOSTOCK HALL Library	0714	10	2334
LEYLAND Fishwicks Garage	......	to	......
LEYLAND The Gables	0723	35	2343
LEYLAND Tesco Store	0726	mins	2346
MOSS SIDE Black Bull	0734	until	2354
LEYLAND Fishwicks Garage	0740		2400

LEYLAND - PENWORTHAM - PRESTON   111
Saturday

LEYLAND Fishwicks Garage	0615		2230
MOSS SIDE Black Bull	0621	then	2236
LEYLAND St.Andrews Way (Tesco)	0629	every	2244
LEYLAND opp The Gables	0632	10	2247
LEYLAND Station Brow	0634	to	2249
LOSTOCK HALL Library	0641	35	2256
PENWORTHAM New Lane	0645	mins	2300
PRESTON Opp Railway Station	0650	until	2305
PRESTON Bus Station	0655		2310

PRESTON - PENWORTHAM - LEYLAND   111
Sunday

PRESTON Bus Station [76]	1020		2315
PRESTON Fishergate	1024	then	2319
PENWORTHAM New Lane	1029	every	2324
LEYLAND Station Brow	1034	30	2329
LEYLAND Gables	1043	to	2338
LEYLAND Tesco Store	1046	50	2341
MOSS SIDE Black Bull	1054	mins	2349
LEYLAND Fishwicks Garage	1100	until	2355

LEYLAND - PENWORTHAM - PRESTON   111
Sunday

LEYLAND Fishwicks Garage	0930		2230
MOSS SIDE Black Bull	0936	then	2236
LEYLAND St.Andrews Way (Tesco)	0944	every	2244
LEYLAND opp The Gables	0947	30	2247
LEYLAND Station Brow	0949	to	2249
TARDY GATE Pleasant Retreat	0956	50	2256
PENWORTHAM New Lane	1000	mins	2300
PRESTON Opp Railway Station	1005	until	2305
PRESTON Bus Station	1010		2310

PRESTON - LEYLAND - CHORLEY   109
Monday to Friday
Running every 10 - 65 mins dependent on school/college hours

PRESTON Bus Station [75]		0800	to	1710
PRESTON Fishergate Yorks BS		0804	to	1714
PENWORTHAM New Lane		0809	to	1719
LOSTOCK HALL Library		0816	to	1726
LEYLAND Fishwicks Garage	0625	to	0800	
LEYLAND Station Brow		0824	to	1734
LEYLAND The Gables	0629	to	1736
LEYLAND Tesco Store	0632	to	1739
EUXTON Buckshaw Village	0638	to	1745
EUXTON Bay Horse Hotel	0643	to	1750
EUXTON The Talbot	0646	to	1753
CHORLEY Interchange [G]	0653	to	1800

CHORLEY - LEYLAND - PRESTON   109
Monday to Friday
Running every 10 - 65 mins dependent on school/college hours

CHORLEY Interchange	0700		1810
EUXTON The Talbot	0707		1817
EUXTON Bay Horse Hotel	0710	and	1820
EUXTON Buckshaw Village	0715	every	1825
LEYLAND St Andrews Way	0721	10	1831
LEYLAND opp The Gables	0724	to	1834
LEYLAND Station Brow	0726	65	1731
LOSTOCK HALL Library	0734	mins	1739
PENWORTHAM New Lane	0741	until	1746
PRESTON Opp Railway Station	0746		1751
PRESTON Bus Station	0750		1755

PRESTON - LEYLAND - CHORLEY   109
Saturday

PRESTON Bus Station [75]	......	......	0800	every	1705
PRESTON Fishergate Yorks BS	......	......	0804	60	1709
PENWORTHAM New Lane	......	......	0809	mins	1714
LOSTOCK HALL Library	......	......	0816	until	1721
LEYLAND Fishwicks Garage	0625	0715			
LEYLAND Station Brow	......	......	0824		1729
LEYLAND The Gables	0629	0719	0826	and	1731
LEYLAND Tesco Store	0632	0722	0829	every	1734
EUXTON Buckshaw Village	0638	0728	0835	60	1740
EUXTON Bay Horse Hotel	0643	0733	0840	mins	1745
EUXTON The Talbot	0646	0736	0843	until	1748
CHORLEY Interchange [G]	0653	0743	0850		1755

CHORLEY - LEYLAND - PRESTON   109
Saturday

CHORLEY Interchange	0700		1810
EUXTON The Talbot	0707		1817
EUXTON Bay Horse Hotel	0710	and	1820
EUXTON Buckshaw Village	0715	every	1825
LEYLAND St Andrews Way	0721	60	1831
LEYLAND opp The Gables	0724	mins	1834
LEYLAND Station Brow	0726	until	1836
LOSTOCK HALL Library	0734		1739
PENWORTHAM New Lane	0741		1746
PRESTON Opp Railway Station	0746		1751
PRESTON Bus Station	0750		1755

PRESTON - LEYLAND - CHORLEY   109
Sunday

PRESTON Bus Station [75]	......	1100	1300	1500	1700
PRESTON Fishergate Yorks BS	......	1104	1304	1504	1704
PENWORTHAM New Lane	......	1109	1309	1509	1709
LOSTOCK HALL Library	......	1116	1316	1516	1716
LEYLAND Station Brow	......	1123	1323	1523	1723
LEYLAND Fishwicks Garage	0920	......	......	......	......
LEYLAND The Gables	0925	1125	1325	1525	1725
LEYLAND Tesco Store	0928	1128	1328	1528	1728
EUXTON Buckshaw Village	0934	1134	1334	1534	1734
EUXTON Bay Horse Hotel	0939	1139	1339	1539	1739
EUXTON The Talbot	0941	1141	1341	1541	1741
CHORLEY Interchange [G]	0948	1148	1348	1548	1748

CHORLEY - LEYLAND - PRESTON   109
Sunday

CHORLEY Interchange	0950	1150	1350	1550	1750
EUXTON The Talbot	0957	1157	1357	1557	1757
EUXTON Bay Horse Hotel	0959	1159	1359	1559	1759
EUXTON Buckshaw Village	1004	1204	1404	1604	1804
LEYLAND St Andrews Way	1010	1210	1410	1610	1810
LEYLAND opp The Gables	1013	1213	1413	1612	1813
LEYLAND Fishwicks Garage	......	......	......	1614	......
LEYLAND Station Brow	1015	1215	1415	1616	......
LOSTOCK HALL Library	1022	1222	1422	1622	......
PENWORTHAM New Lane	1029	1229	1429	1629	......
PRESTON Opp Railway Station	1034	1234	1434	1634	......
PRESTON Bus Station	1038	1238	1438	1638	......

PRESTON - PENWORTHAM - MOSS SIDE - LEYLAND - CHORLEY   115
Monday to Friday

PRESTON Bus Station [77]	0750	0750		0855		1555	1705
PRESTON Fishergate Yorks BS	0754	0754		0859		1559	1709
PENWORTHAM Plough Inn	0805	0805	0810	0910		1610	1720
WHITESTAKE Corner	0808	0808	0813	0913	and	1613	1723
FARINGTON jct Church Ln/Croston Rd	0812	0812	0817	0917	every	1617	1727
EARNSHAW BRIDGE Leyland Tiger	0816	0816	0821	0921	60	1621	1731
MOSS SIDE Black Bull	0821	0821	0826	0926	mins	1626	1736
LEYLAND Seven Stars	0824	0824	0829	0929	until	1629	1739
LEYLAND Tesco Store	0827	0827	0832	0932		1632	1742
LEYLAND Gables							1745
LEYLAND Fishwicks Garage							1750
LEYLAND Runshaw College	0830	0830	0835	0935		1635	
EUXTON Euxton Lane Runshaw AEC		0837		0942		1642	
CHORLEY Hospital		0840		0945		1645	
CHORLEY Interchange [F]		0845		0950		1650	

CHORLEY - LEYLAND - MOSS SIDE - PENWORTHAM - PRESTON   115
Monday to Friday

CHORLEY Interchange			0910	1000			1710
CHORLEY Hospital			0915	1005			1715
EUXTON Euxton Lane Runshaw AEC			0918	1008			1718
LEYLAND Runshaw College			0925	1015	and	1635	1725
LEYLAND Fishwicks Garage	0700	0800			every		
LEYLAND Gables	0702	0802			60		
LEYLAND opp Library	0705	0805	0928	1018	mins	1638	1728
LEYLAND Seven Stars	0708	0808	0931	1021	until	1641	1731
MOSS SIDE Black Bull	0711	0811	0934	1024		1644	1734
EARNSHAW BRIDGE Leyland Tiger	0716	0816	0939	1029		1649	1738
LEYLAND Fishwicks Garage							1740
FARINGTON jct Church Ln/Croston Rd	0720	0820	0943	1033		1653	
WHITESTAKE Corner	0724	0824	0947	1037		1657	
PENWORTHAM Plough Inn	0727	0827	0950	1040		1700	
PRESTON Opp Railway Station	0738	0838	1001	1051		1711	
PRESTON Bus Station [77]	0742	0842	1005	1055		1715	

PRESTON - MOSS SIDE - LEYLAND   115
Saturday

PRESTON Bus Station [77]	0900		1705
PRESTON Fishergate Yorks BS	0904		1709
PENWORTHAM Plough Inn	0915	and	1720
WHITESTAKE Corner	0918	every	1723
FARINGTON jct Church Ln/Croston Rd	0922	60	1727
EARNSHAW BRIDGE Leyland Tiger	0926	mins	1731
MOSS SIDE Black Bull	0931	until	1736
LEYLAND Seven Stars	0935		1740
LEYLAND Library	0940		1745
LEYLAND opp The Gables	0942		1747
LEYLAND Fishwicks Garage	0945		1750

LEYLAND - MOSS SIDE - PRESTON   115
Saturday

LEYLAND Fishwicks Garage	0805		1605
LEYLAND The Gables	0807		1607
LEYLAND Library	0810	and	1610
LEYLAND Seven Stars	0815	every	1615
MOSS SIDE Black Bull	0819	60	1619
EARNSHAW BRIDGE Leyland Tiger	0824	mins	1624
FARINGTON jct Church Ln/Croston Rd	0828	until	1628
WHITESTAKE Corner	0832		1632
PENWORTHAM Plough Inn	0835		1635
PRESTON Opp Railway Station	0846		1646
PRESTON Bus Station [77]	0850		1650

John Fishwick & Sons   TIMETABLES 2007   Routes 116, 117 & 119

LEYLAND - MOSS SIDE - PRESTON   116
Monday to Friday

LEYLAND Fishwicks Garage	0740	......	......	......	......
LEYLAND Seven Stars St Annes sch	0751	0851	0951	1051	1151
MOSS SIDE Black Bull	0755	0855	0955	1055	1155
EARNSHAW BRIDGE Leyland Tiger	0800	0900	1000	1100	1200
FARINGTON jct Church Ln/Croston Rd	0804	0904	1004	1104	1204
TARDY GATE Croston Road	0808	0908	1008	1108	1208
PRESTON Opp Railway Station	0819	0919	1019	1119	1219
PRESTON Bus Station	0823	0923	1023	1123	1223

PRESTON - MOSS SIDE - LEYLAND   116
Monday to Friday

LEYLAND Seven Stars St Annes sch	0851	0951	1051	1151
MOSS SIDE Black Bull	0855	0955	1055	1155
EARNSHAW BRIDGE Leyland Tiger	0900	1000	1100	1200
FARINGTON jct Church Ln/Croston Rd	0904	1004	1104	1204
TARDY GATE Croston Road	0908	1008	1108	1208
PRESTON Opp Railway Station	0919	1019	1119	1219
PRESTON Bus Station	0923	1023	1123	1223

PRESTON - LEYLAND VIA BAMBER BRIDGE   117
Monday to Friday

PRESTON Bus Station [75]	0745	1030	1230	1430	1630
PRESTON Fishergate Yorks BS	0749	1034	1234	1434	1634
PENWORTHAM New Lane	0754	1039	1239	1439	1639
TARDY GATE Wateringpool Lane	0759	1044	1244	1444	1644
BAMBER BRIDGE Railway Station	0805	1050	1250	1450	1650
CLAYTON BROOK Village Centre	0812	1057	1257	1457	1657
LANCASTER LANE Hayrick Inn	0821	1106	1306	1506	1706
LEYLAND The Gables	0826	1111	1311	1511	1711
LEYLAND Tesco Store	0829	1114	1314	1514	1714
MOSS SIDE Black Bull	0838	1123	1323	1523	1723
LEYLAND Fishwicks Garage	0845	1130	1330	1530	1730

LEYLAND - PRESTON VIA BAMBER BRIDGE   117
Monday to Friday

LEYLAND Fishwicks Garage	0725	0925	1125	1325	1525
MOSS SIDE Black Bull	0733	0933	1133	1333	1533
LEYLAND TESCO	0742	0942	1142	1342	1542
LEYLAND Gables Hotel	0745	0945	1145	1345	1545
LANCASTER LANE Hayrick Inn	0749	0949	1149	1349	1549
CLAYTON BROOK Village Centre	0758	0958	1158	1358	1558
BAMBER BRIDGE Railway Station	0805	1005	1205	1405	1605
TARDY GATE Wateringpool Lane	0811	1011	1211	1411	1611
PENWORTHAM New Lane	0815	1015	1215	1415	1615
PRESTON opp Railway Station	0821	1021	1221	1421	1621
PRESTON Bus Station	0825	1025	1225	1425	1625

PRESTON - LEYLAND VIA BAMBER BRIDGE   117
Saturday

PRESTON Bus Station [75]	1030	1230	1430	1630
PRESTON Fishergate Yorks BS	1034	1234	1434	1634
PENWORTHAM New Lane	1039	1239	1439	1639
TARDY GATE Wateringpool Lane	1044	1244	1444	1644
BAMBER BRIDGE Railway Station	1050	1250	1450	1650
CLAYTON BROOK Village Centre	1057	1257	1457	1657
LANCASTER LANE Hayrick Inn	1106	1306	1506	1706
LEYLAND The Gables	1111	1311	1511	1711
LEYLAND Tesco Store	1114	1314	1514	1714
MOSS SIDE Black Bull	1123	1323	1523	1723
LEYLAND Fishwicks Garage	1130	1330	1530	1730

LEYLAND - PRESTON VIA BAMBER BRIDGE   117
Saturday

LEYLAND Fishwicks Garage	0725	0925	1125	1325	1525
MOSS SIDE Black Bull	0732	0932	1132	1332	1532
LEYLAND Tesco Store	0741	0941	1141	1341	1541
LEYLAND opp The Gables	0744	0944	1144	1344	1544
LANCASTER LANE Hayrick Inn	0749	0949	1149	1349	1549
CLAYTON BROOK Village Centre	0758	0958	1158	1358	1558
BAMBER BRIDGE Railway Station	0805	1005	1205	1405	1605
TARDY GATE Wateringpool Lane	0811	1011	1211	1411	1611
PENWORTHAM New Lane	0815	1015	1215	1415	1615
PRESTON Opp Railway Station	0820	1020	1220	1420	1620
PRESTON Bus Station	0825	1025	1225	1425	1625

PRESTON - LEYLAND – CHORLEY   119
Monday to Friday

LEYLAND Fishwicks Garage	0755	0900	......	1600	1700
LEYLAND The Gables	0758	0903	......	1603	1703
LEYLAND Runshaw College	0802	0907	1635	1607	1707
EUXTON Bay Horse Hotel	0807	0912	1640	1612	1712
CHORLEY Hospital	0811	0916	1649	1616	1716
CHORLEY Interchange [G]	0816	0921	1654	1621	1721

CHORLEY - LEYLAND – PRESTON   119
Monday to Friday

CHORLEY Interchange	0825	0820	0930	1730
CHORLEY Hospital	0830	0825	0935	1735
EUXTON Bay Horse Hotel	0834	0829	0939	1739
LEYLAND Runshaw College	0839	0834	0944	1744
LEYLAND The Gables	0843	......	0948	1748
LEYLAND Fishwicks Garage	0846	......	0951	1751

PRESTON - LEYLAND – CHORLEY   119
Saturday

LEYLAND Fishwicks Garage	0900	1000	1100	1200	1300	1400	1500
LEYLAND The Gables	0903	1003	1103	1203	1303	1403	1503
LEYLAND Runshaw College	0907	1007	1107	1207	1307	1407	1507
EUXTON Bay Horse Hotel	0912	1012	1112	1212	1312	1412	1512
CHORLEY Hospital	0916	1016	1116	1216	1316	1416	1516
CHORLEY Interchange [G]	0921	1021	1121	1221	1321	1421	1521

CHORLEY - LEYLAND – PRESTON   119
Saturday

CHORLEY Interchange	0930	1030	1130	1230	1330	1430	1530
CHORLEY Hospital	0935	1035	1135	1235	1335	1435	1535
EUXTON Bay Horse Hotel	0939	1039	1139	1239	1339	1439	1539
LEYLAND Runshaw College	0944	1044	1144	1244	1344	1444	1544
LEYLAND The Gables	0948	1048	1148	1248	1348	1448	1548
LEYLAND Fishwicks Garage	0951	1051	1151	1251	1351	1451	1551

PICTORIAL VIEW

*Leyland 'X' Type, B5783 which was used as a wagon weekdays and converted for use as a bus at weekends,
as seen complete with canvas roof.*

*A line of Leyland N. B8851 and A9 vehicles at the terminus in Corporation Street,
prior to operating from the Fox Street bus station, which was sited to the rear of the vehicles.
Note Singletons vehicle in the foreground of similar type, TE6317*

No17, TE9307 the last of the five Leyland TS2's to be delivered in 1929

PICTORIAL VIEW

Rear view of Leyland TD4 after completion of Burlingham part of bodywork prior to delivery to Fishwicks. No6, ATD776.

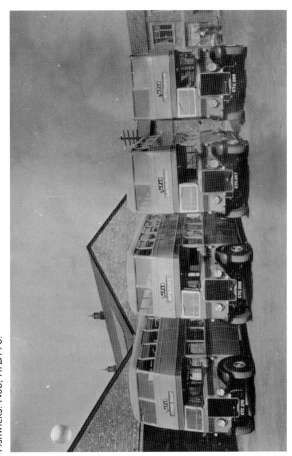

The four Leyland TD5 with lowbridge Burlingham body's on arrival at Fishwicks. Nos18-21, CTC267-70.

No 2, TF5919 an all Leyland TD1 seen in Fox Street bus station prior to its return journey to Leyland.

Double deck Leyland TD1 and TD4's with Leyland PLSC and LT9 Lions circa 1939/40.

PICTORIAL VIEW

Low and highbridge all Leyland PD2's parked in the yard adjacent to the garage. No 23, LTD445 & No6, TTB973.

Rear offside view of Leyland highbridge PD2 - No6, TTB973 in Fox Street bus station.

All Leyland, No26, JTJ824, PD1 with highbridge bodywork in Fishergate, Preston on its return journey to Leyland.

A Leyland PD2 - No3, NTD425 and a PD1 - No33, GTF283 both with Leyland lowbridge bodywork.

524 CTF IN ITS FOUR GUISES - *Two of the single deck Leyland Olympians were converted to coach specification, one was originally No29, which became C5 in coach livery then on return to bus duties became No22, 524CTF. After Fishwicks it passed to Leyland Paints.*

PICTORIAL VIEW

Rear view of two Leyland PD2, after addition of rear doors Nos21 & 20, and two Atlantean's Nos24 & 31, all with Weymann bodywork along with front of Atlantean/ Alexander No34.

One of the two 49 seat Weymann bodied Leyland Leopard's seen entering the new Preston bus station. No28. CTB952B.

Eight Leyland Olympic integral single deck vehicles arrived between March and November 1951. No16. NTC233 was one of the second batch.

All with lowbridge Weymann bodywork on Leyland chassis are two Atlantean PDR's 24 &30, ATB596/7A and Titan PD2 No20, 531CTF

PICTORIAL VIEW

Yard View circa 1965

The ex demonstrator Leyland Panther with Park Royal body, also entering Preston bus station, prior to being converted to single door was numbered 1, JTJ667F.

No34, SGD669 another ex demonstration vehicle to be acquired was this Leyland Atlantean with Alexander bodywork seen between the railway bridges at Lostock Hall on service to Preston.

Three of the seven Weymann lowbridge bodied Leyland Atlanteans Nos 25/6/35, TTE641-3D

PICTORIAL VIEW

The first full size vehicle out of Fowlers bodyshop, for Fishwicks was this Leyland PDR Atlantean No6, MTE186K.

Fowler bodies, between 1970 and 1974 were also mounted on Leyland Leopard and Diamler Fleetline chassis. No 16 BTD779J was one of the three Leopards and Nos 10 & 9, WTE485/ 4L were two of the five Daimlers.

The first vehicle, for Fishwick, after acquisition of Fowlers bodybuilders was this 12 coach seated Ford Transit C11, LTE286F.

PICTORIAL VIEW

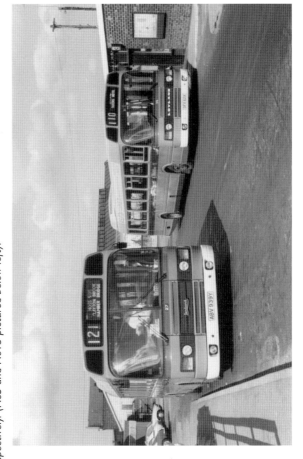

Leyland produced National Mk1 in three lengths - 11.3, 10.9 and 10.3. Fishwicks operated examples of each. No4, HCW461N / No 13, TLS733P ex demonstrator and No3, PTC123M ex Lancaster, each type respectively. (No5 and No13 pictured below left).

Two of the eight Mk2 Nationals on layover at Tuer Street. Last to arrive No 27, ABV939Y and to the right No 26, OFX621X.

PICTORIAL VIEW

Four variations of Plaxton bodywork delivered between 1973 and 1983 were (top LHS)C3, BTB779L Leopard/Elite unknown location, (top RHS) C9, GRN259S Leopard with Supreme bodywork seen in Manchester (bot LHS) C4, TRN91X Tiger / Viewmaster bodywork on Preston bus station and (bot RHS). C5, LSB83 Tiger / Paramount bodywork at Worden Park for a Leyland publicity shot

PICTORIAL VIEW

No2, A462LFV was originally a Leyland prototype chassis, acquired by Fishwicks it received an ECW Olympian type body and is at Leyland test track on special service duties at the Leyland 90 celebration.

Only two Bova Futura's were operated by the company, unfortunately after Fishwicks this one was stolen and caught fire. C10, F550YCW.

One of the three Leyland B15/ PRV prototype vehicles about to take the turning into Tuer street was No25, NHG732P.

One of five DAF vehicles operating from 1987 with Van Hool Alizee bodywork was C15, D277XCX.

PICTORIAL VIEW

Rear view of one of four Freight Rover Sherpa/ Optare ex Yorkshire Rider minis acquired for commencement of Fishkwick services around Leyland. M1, D703HUA

M10, E100MFV a Mercedes / Reeves Burgess which became the favoured combination for the mini fleet.

The last two of the eight Mercedes / Reeves Burgess mini buses, M1/2, F705/6WFV.

PICTORIAL VIEW

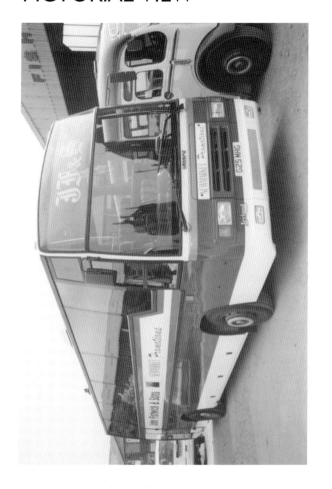

Four more examples of Plaxton bodywork. Paramounts (top LHS) C7, F57YCW a Leyland Tiger in Llandindrod Wells. (top RHS) C5, G25MHG Leyland Tiger operating for Newmarket Promotions and (bottom) two ex Parks Volvo B10M's – C12, F973HGE and C6, G53RGG.

PICTORIAL VIEW

Leyland Lynx, replacement for the National, was produced in two versions, Fishwicks operated four of each. No25, D25VCW a Mk I version and three of the Mk2 versions No14, J14JFS / No 3, J7JFS and at the rear No 4or5, H64/5CCK.

M665WCK, one of the two Volvo B10M's with Plaxton Excalibur bodywork operating for FourWinds travel.

Two Ex Thamesdown Daimler Fleetline/ ECW double deck were acquired in 1993 to cover additional school contract work. No17, UMR196T

PICTORIAL VIEW

Double deck Leyland Atlantean's, Bristol VRT's and Daimler Fleetlines, circa 1994

Three DAF SB3000 with Van Hool Alizee bodywork in all different liveries. R61/2 GNW & T58AUA.

One of the four, short term loan DAF SB220 with Northern Counties body's. Allocated briefly No13 was M850RCP. Note Mr Brindle ensuring the vehicle is in suitable condition for service.

Single deck Mk1 and Mk2 National's, Mk2 Lynx and Dennis Dart's, circa 1997

No1, L1JFS a DAF SB120 with Wright Cadet bodywork was exhibited in the 1999 Bus & Coach Show prior to arriving at Fishwicks.

No1, L1JFS a DAF SB120 with Wright Cadet bodywork was exhibited in the 1999 Bus & Coach Show prior to arriving at Fishwicks.

No35, R32GNW a Northern Counties bodied DAF SB220, rear view seen in Fishwick livery

One of six ECW bodied Bristol VRT's acquired for school contracts is seen on Preston bus station was No13, EAP988V.

Seen in Hough Lane, Leyland initially on loan is No35, R32GNW a Northern Counties bodied DAF SB220, later after purchase, rear view seen in Fishwick livery

PICTORIAL VIEW

*No38, X823NWX one of three more DAF SB120 / Wright Cadets commencing service
early 2001 seen leaving Chorley bus station*

*Four of the DAF SB120's with Wright bodywork
Nos38/37/1 &36, X823/2NWX, L1JFS & X821NWX*

*The DAF SB200 with Wright Commander bodies became a favoured combination,
eight being purchased between 2002 & 05 shown is No10, YJ53VDT.*

PICTORIAL VIEW

Bristol VRT's with ECW bodywork Nos 24 / 13 & 29, LFJ879W, EAP988V & AAP651T

Ex Preston AN68's with Alexander bodywork Nos 22 / 20 & 13, UHG149/50/47V

Ex Lothian Olympian's with Alexander bodywork Nos 32/4/3, F352/5/3WSC

Three rear views of the various livery's between 1998 and 2006 seen on DAF SB3000 - R61GNW in Bournmouth, EOS90 Y478HUA at Aintree Race Course and DAF SB4000 YJ06LGA in Strencham services.

PICTORIAL VIEW

Various livery changes are seen on EOS – M823RCP and YD02RHF also DAF SB4000 / VH with the Fishwick 'Classic Gold Holidays' Livery, introduced in 2003, is YJ04BJF seen in Stockholm.

Rear nearside view of one of five ex Lothian Alexander bodied Olympian's after conversion to single door. No33, F353WSC.

Two more DAF SB120 with Wright Cadet bodies commenced service on the 2nd January 2005, one was No6. YJ54CFN.

The second DAF SB200 with Plaxton Centro bodywork is No25, YJ07JWE seen along side similar vehicle except with Wright bodywork, on short term loan - YJ07JDZ, temporary No50.

PICTORIAL VIEW

A typical yard view first thing on Sunday morning, prior to commencement of services.

A view of all the types of single deck vehicles operated during Centenary year.

PICTORIAL VIEW - After Fishwicks

The Peoples Church ran Ex No29, DTE459 a Leyland LT9 with Burlingham body, seen in Liverpool.

Leyland single deck Olympian Ex No15, 525CTF with Williams, Llangollen at their depot.

Ex No3, TF5920 - All Leyland Titan TD1 with Progress Motors of Chorley in the early 1950's

All Leyland PD1 - Ex No33, GTF283 with Townson Plant of Bolton.

PICTORIAL VIEW - After Fishwicks

TTE642D, Ex No25 is seen with Rennies of Dunfermline.

Preston North End FC acquired Leopard / Plaxton Ex C5, VTC716H in 1982, re registered A61ABM, seen outside the football ground.

Grayline, Clackmannan Scotland, operated Ex No33, STC359C the dual purpose Leopard / MCW.

Ex C9, 750TJ one of the two Leyland Leopards with Duple Dragonfly body passed to Rennies then to Stirling Rowing Club and is seen complete with roof mounted boats in one of the service areas returning to base.

PICTORIAL VIEW - After Fishwicks

Ex No22. SRN103P now converted to a mobil music centre in South Cumbria an AN68 with East Lancs body.

One of the short National I's, which was originally from Lancaster, seen with GL Travel, Winsford ex No5, PTC124M.

Longer version of the Leopard / Plaxton Elite, Ex C2, BTB778L - seen outside the authors house on-looked by daughter in 1986 - after passing to Maypole, Burscough.

Seen in Accrington town centre after removal of roof heating pod is one of the National I's in Pilkingtons revised livery PIL8076 - Ex No29, XCW957R.

LIL5069 a DAF / Plaxton Paramount operating with United Welsh, seen in Port Talbot on the last day of last century - Ex C7. C792MVH.

Ex C6. E346EVH a DAF / Van Hool with Elizabethan, Bloxwich and re registered A17ETL.

One of the three Ex Leyland Titan prototypes - No20. FHG592S, passed to Kerygma Trust, Hawick where it seen in June 1999.

One of the two Leyland Royal Tigers Ex C12. C753MFR now with Lakeland Commercials, Kendal seen on Tebay Services in June 2001.

PICTORIAL VIEW - After Fishwicks

Another mini Ex M1, F705WFV with Tyne Blue Line, Northumberland on layover in Newcastle.

Galloway of Suffolk. leaving Victoria Interchange on National Express duties, 1482PP a Van Hool bodied DAF SB3000 Ex J9JFS.

M711HUA, Ex M2 Freight Rover / Optare with Darwen Coach Services seen in Blackburn 1993.

A16BUS a Volvo B10M with Plaxton Paramount body seen June 2006 in London operating with West's of Woodford Green was Ex F972HGE.

PICTORIAL VIEW - After Fishwicks

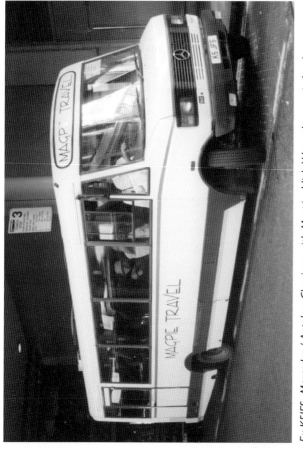

Ex K5JFS Mercedes / Autobus Classique with Magpie, High Wycombe seen in London.

Three of the ECW bodied Bristol VRT's passed to Alphine Llandudno, Ex No20, LUA714V seen in the Llandudno yard.

Now in Malta with Supreme, Ex K3JFS re registered ACY911, one of the two Volvo / Plaxton Premiers.

With a local company, John Bretherton of Chipping is EOS 90 Ex L1JFS now registered G1GLT.

PICTORIAL VIEW - After Fishwicks

W224CDN an EOS 90 seen at Quantocks garage in Somerset 2005, but now with Butlers of Kirby in Ashfield seen re - registered 179BUT in Chichester, November 2006.

Ex No29, T154AUA is now with Elite Travel, Carlton and is seen on Poulton bus station prior to its journey to Cleveleys in August 2005.

Kimes of Folkingham now operate two of the four DAF SB220 / Northern Counties, PAZ9346 Ex No36, M848RCP is seen leaving Stamford bus station en route to Peterborough.

PICTORIAL VIEW - Then and Now

View circa early 1920's of the original terminus point in Preston, Corporation Street near rear of Public Hall site – Leyland S5's and A9's.

Similar view of site in 2007.

View seen through entrance, from Corporation Street, circa early 60's into Fox Street bus station - Highbridge Leyland PD2 No6.

Similar view of site in 2007.

View from Fox Sreet of bus station circa mid 1950's - Leyland PS1 / Burlingham No7 awaiting return journey to Leyland. Note narrow entry towards RHS.

Similar view of site in 2007.

PICTORIAL VIEW - Preserved Vehicles histories since departure from Fishwicks

No7   521CTF
1957   Leyland Olympian
Weymann single deck body
New 10/57
In Service 01/11/57
Withdrawn 26/03/73
Sold 03/73
03/73 Sold to Hollis, Queensferry.
Passed to Williams, t/a Haydn, Chirk,
by 08/75 Passed to Warstone, t/a Green Bus,
Gt Wyrley, Fleet number 14.
05/93 Acquired by Mark Hayes, Leyland,
for preservation.

No5   528CTF   1958
Leyland PD2/40 Titan
Weymann lowbridge body
New 02/58
In Service 11/03/58
Withdrawn 21/03/78
Sold 05/78
75/76 Used as a driver training vehicle as
well as a service bus.
05/78 Sold to Rennie, Dunfermline.
03/81 Passed to Stocks, haulage
contractor/preservationist, Kincardine.
Re-sold to a church group in South Wales a
few months later.
14/12/81 Passed to John Jarvis, converted to
mobile/static home, Cynwil Elfed,
Carmarthen, South Wales.
06/03/92 Acquired by W Ashcroft
for preservation - Fully restored to original
Fishwick condition and livery.
Started attending rallies in late 1996.

No12 VTD441H 1970
Leyland Tiger Cub PSUC1/12
Fowler single deck body
New 27/01/70
In Service 31/03/70
Withdrawn 20/04/78
Sold 04/78
04/78 Sold to Phillips Motor Services,
Holywell, Clwyd.
08/84 Eagles and Hughes, Mold.
05/85 Parish, Hawarden, - Livery Red.
08/89 Stewart, t/a South Lancs Transport,
St Helens.
01/91 Purchased by Mark Hayes, Leyland,
for Preservation.

PICTORIAL VIEW - Wagons by the late Don Threlfall

Another Leyland Wagon was No 22 – TE1014 a SWQ2 'special' having three axles, new in 1927, note haulage vehicles still with solid tyres well into the twenties.

The last vehicles to arrive for the haulage fleet, in 1933/4, were three Leyland TSC9 Beavers which often were seen with draw bar trailers. Nos 8,9 &10 – TJ2813, TJ4391 & TJ3991 respectively

No 17 – TC6272 a Leyland SQH2 and No 21 – TD7271 a SQ2, two of the early haulage fleet vehicles, 1924 & 1926 respectively.

Ex demonstration vehicle, No 11 – TJ31 was a Leyland Bull TSQ2, new to Fishwick in 1934.

PICTORIAL VIEW - Buses by the late Don Threlfall

The first single deck vehicles after the war were Leyland PS1's again with Burlingham bodies. No 8 – HTE954 was one of six to arrive between 1946-9.

Rear view of No16 – TC6093, one of four Leyland A9 known within the company as 'The Whippet's', as they were much faster than other vehicles on the road at that time. 1923/4.

Two of the four LT9 Lions with Burlingham bodies which were the last vehicles delivered prior to the second world war in early 1939. Nos 29 & 31 – DTE458/60

An example of the Leyland PLSC Lion, one of seventeen, is No 23 – TE1694 new in 1927.

One PLSC3 Lions, No 11 – TE4621, was commandeered during the second world war and used as an ambulance.

PICTORIAL VIEW

One of the eight Leyland Olympic's was MTD514. No10 seen heading for Leyland.

Chapel Brow coach garage with Leyland Leopard's, C1.7587TF the coach with Dragonfly bodywork and No33, STC359C with Weymann Dual purpose bodywork in bus livery.

All Leyland lowbridge PD2 - No23, LTD423 seen prior to return to Leyland on Croston Road service.

Altogether eight Leyland PDR Atlantean's with MCW/ Weymann lowbridge bodywork were operated, No26, TTE642D is seen entering Preston at the Railway station.

Again at Chapel Brow garage, present are C6, RTD432C Leyland Leopard / Plaxton Panorama, C2, 7588TF Albion Victor / Duple Firefly bodywork and C8,YTC794D Bedford J2 / Duple – Willowbrook bodywork.

Leyland National 1 – No1, NFR558T one of three delivered 1979 in revised livery seen leaving Preston bus station.

No3, YTE952D one of two Massey bodied Leyland Tiger Cub's, new in 1966. Seen leaving Chorley Bus Station.

C6, AHG947R Leyland Leopard with Plaxton Supreme bodywork seen in Manchester.

FHG592S. No20 Leyland / PRV B15 seen in demonstration livery prior to purchase by Fishwicks.

No14, J14JFS one of the four Mk2 Leyland Lynx's seen at Tardy Gate.

Seen in Hough Lane, Leyland is Leyland National 2 – No10, WRN412V on the main 111 route to Preston.

One of the early DAF / Van Hool coaches was E320EVH. C14 seen at Chapel Brow garage.

PICTORIAL VIEW

Five ex Preston Leyland AN68 with Alexander bodies replaced the VRT's, No21, UHG144V seen revisiting Preston bus station.

Another example of the Alexander bodied Olympian, offside view of No30, G802GSX, seen on 111 route entering Preston Bus Station at the end of the journey from Leyland.

Parked on Preston bus station, on layover, is No19, R848VEC one of four Wright bodied Dennis Darts.

DAF SB200 /Wright Commander 28, YJ55KZP leaving Tuer Street garage prior to starting duties on the 109 route early on a Sunday morning.

DAF SB3000 / VH Alizee - R61GNW in Dawlish, EOS 90 – seen prior to delivery being registered N662NCW, another EOS W223CDN one of the two for the 2000 season, seen on tour in Bournemouth and DAF SB4000 /Van Hool Alizee with Leger Silver Service Livery is YJ04BYF.

PICTORIAL VIEW

Front nearside view of No24, YJ07JWD, the new DAF SB200 with Plaxton Centro body.

The authors collection of Fishwick vehicles except in 4mm scale!

YJ07JWF, one of the two DAF SB4000/Van Hool Coaches, on arrival end February for '07 tour season

One of the two short Leyland Leopard / Plaxton coaches, ex C4, VTC715H was converted to a breakdown vehicle by Ashtree coaches.

Two of the lowbridge Weymann bodied Atlanteans operated in Canada, with Gray Line Sightseeing Tours, one of them was Ex No25, TTE641D still displaying a local destination. The second one Ex No35, TTE643D, was used on the Oak Bay Explorer route c1997.

One of the six Leyland PD2's with MCW /Weymann bodies Ex No4 - 527CTF seen in Morris Bros yard Swansea.

PICTORIAL VIEW

DAF SB3000 / Van Hool Alizee , Ex N985FWT now with Jones of Flint and re-registered 770HDM seen in Manchester.

Seen in St. Annes June 07, was YJ03PDV a DAF SB4000 / VH Alizee T9 now with Dalesman of Guisley.

Four of the MkI Leyland Nationals passed to MTL Manchester, ex No14, PCK193P was one of them.

Several vehicles have been purchased by Irish operators. Ex C5 - G25MHG was one now with Reddins of Muff re registered 98DL6262.

PICTORIAL VIEW - Preserved Vehicles histories since departure from Fishwicks

No18 XTB728N
1974 Leyland Atlantean AN68
East Lancs highbridge body
New 18/07/74
In Service 01/08/74
Withdrawn 19/06/97
Sold 20/06/97
03/89-09/90 Placed in store at Chapel Brow.
20/06/97 Purchased by M Hayes,
Leyland - for preservation.

No19 XTB729N
1974 Leyland Atlantean AN68
East Lancs highbridge body
New 19/07/74
In Service 01/08/74
Withdrawn 19/06/97
Sold 20/06/97
03/89-09/90
Placed in store at Chapel Brow.
20/06/97 Purchased by M Hayes,
Leyland - for preservation.

No24 XCW955R
1977 Leyland National Mk1
New 11/01/77
In Service 13/01/78
Withdrawn 11/05/95
Sold 12/99
01/77-01/78 Delivered in all over white,
used as Demonstrator by LMLtd.
11/84 Repainted with broader green waist
band, revised style fleet names
`JOHN FISHWICK & SONS`
and JF&S scroll on front panel.
05/95 In store Chapel Brow.
12/99 Acquired by W. Ashcroft
for Preservation.

No3 BCK706R
1977 Leyland Titan (prototype)
Park Royal / Leyland body
New 09/11/82   In Service 01/12/82
Withdrawn 20/11/86   Sold 21/11/86
1977 Built as Leyland Test /Demonstration
vehicle - B15 05. Seating H44/27D
LTE initial assessment vehicle.
11/82 Painted into Fishwick livery. Seating
converted to H44/27F.
11/86 Ensign Bus, Purfleet, London. Fleet
No H106.
--/87 On loan to Southern Vectus, t/a
Southern Blue Line
--/-- University Bus, Hatfield. Re registered
VLT240 then TMR535R.
11/95 Cherry, Bootle t/a Aintree Coachlines.
08/96 Acquired by Mark Hayes, Leyland,
for Preservation.
05/97 Re registered BCK706R.
03/05-06/07 Re paneled and Re painted
Fishwick livery

Fleet No	Reg No	Chassis Type	Body Type	Chassis No	Body No	Seating	Date In	Date Out	Notes
2	B2247	Leyland Steam Wagon	#/*UECC or Leyland	X101-493		Ch30B	--/07	--/15	Made by LSMC
3	?	Leyland X2 35HP Long	#				c10/10	06/23	I. W 12/25. * Bus body, NAMED 'The Old Rip'.
4	BS5..or B23..	Leyland X2 35HP	#				c06/11	?/14	Possibly acquired by WD during 1914
5	B5783	Leyland X3.40.X2	Leyland	X2-1548		Ch29	c02/13	?/14	NAMED 'The Hanley'. Possibly acquired by WD during 1914
6	B5783	Leyland X4.40.X4	#/Chara	3768		Ch32	c4.5/14	01/34	I. W 01/33 2.S Converted to Chara @w/e, NAMED 'The May Queen'
5	B5951	Leyland Subsidy A	Leyland Sided&Cab/*	3768			--/16	07/35	I. W 07/384 2.S *Converted as required with body from 'The May Queen'
7	B8631	Leyland G or I?	#	9278			--/19	04/39	I. W 04/38 2.S
									(Note: Licensing records show B5951 as the 1st registered of the above two vehicles)
8	B8851	Leyland N	Leyland	10372		B..R	12/19	11/29	I. W 01/33
9	) TB3775	Leyland N ?	Leyland			B...	--/20	12/25	
10	) TB3775	Leyland N ?	Leyland			B...	--/20	12/25	
11	TB6627	Leyland G7 ?	Leyland	12287		B...	07/21	06/28	I. W 04/37
12	TB7414	Leyland G7 ?	Leyland	12248		B...	10/21	05/29	I. W 10/33 2.Dis
13	TC5847	Leyland A9	Leyland	19657		B20F	12/23	05/29	I. H 07/33
14	TC5874	Leyland A9	Leyland	19658		B20F	12/23	05/29	I. H 03/39 2.Hc
15	TC6053	Leyland A9	Leyland	19659		B20F	01/24	06/28	I. H 04/36
16	TC6093	Leyland A9	Leyland	19660		B20F	01/24	05/29	I. H 01/36
17	TC6272	Leyland SQH2	#	15119			01/24	12/33	I.W 01/33 2.S
18	TD5014	Leyland Lion PLSC1	Leyland	45095		B31F	04/26	03/33	I.H 07/40
19	TD5015	Leyland Lion PLSC1	Leyland	45096		B31F	04/26	03/33	I.H 04/39
20	TD5016	Leyland QH2	#	15612			03/26	--/--	I.W 01/46 2.S
21	TD7271	Leyland SQ2	#	15719			07/26	12/35	I.W 01/35 2.S
22	TE1014	Leyland Special SWQ2	#	15912			07/27	12/46	I.W 01/46 2.Bu, S --/--
20	TE1637	Leyland Lion PLSC3	Leyland	45994		B32F	09/27	02/50	I.Sh 06/51
21	TE1636	Leyland Lion PLSC3	Leyland	45995		B32F	09/27	09/33	I.H 10/38 2.S
22	TE1695	Leyland Lion PLSC3	Leyland	46121		B32F	09/27	01/51	I.H 01/51
23	TE1694	Leyland Lion PLSC3	Leyland	46122		B32F	09/27	08/49	I.H --/--
24	TE1834	Leyland Lion PLSC3	Leyland	46280		B32F	10/27	03/48	I.W 07/49 2.S 3.Pn
25	TE2331	Leyland Lion PLSC3	Leyland	46491		B32F	01/28	12/47	I.H 05/49
26	TE2332	Leyland Lion PLSC3	Leyland	46492		B32F	01/28	12/46	I.W 01/61
9	TE4619	Leyland Lion PLSC3	Leyland	47114		B32F	07/28	12/50	I.H 01/51 2.Sc 10/60
10	TE4620	Leyland Lion PLSC3	Leyland	47115		B32F	07/28	03/50	I.Sh 10/50
11	TE4621	Leyland Lion PLSC3	Leyland	47202		B32F	07/28	06/46	I.Pr 06/58 2.A --/39 to --/45
15	TE4622	Leyland Lion PLSC3	Leyland	47203		B32F	07/28	06/47	I.H 10/49
12	TE7865	Leyland Tiger TS2	Leyland	60417		B30F	05/29	07/51	I.H 05/55 Re-seated B33F --/--
13	TE7862	Leyland Tiger TS2	Leyland	60414		B30F	05/29	07/51	I.H 04/52
14	TE7863	Leyland Tiger TS2	Leyland	60415		B30F	05/29	--/52	Oil engine inst. 04/46
16	TE7864	Leyland Tiger TS2	Leyland	60416		B30F	05/29	07/51	I.H 01/52
17	TE9307	Leyland Tiger TS2	Leyland	60540		B30F	09/29	07/51	I.Sh 07/51
5	TD9703	Leyland Lion PLSC1	Leyland	45658		B31F	10/30	05/51	I.W 01/53 3.E 4.Y 2.W --/34 Re-numbered 6
6	TE909	Leyland Lion PLSC1	Leyland	45864		B32F	10/30	05/33	I.W 10/50 2.S 3.B 4.Y
7	TE1998	Leyland Lion PLSC3	Leyland	46358		B32F	10/30	01/39	I.H 01/38 2.Bu --/39 3.Y 4.Y
8	TE1794	Leyland Lion PLSC3	Leyland	46152		B32F	10/30	03/47	I.H 04/49 3.Y 4.Y
1	TF5921	Leyland Titan TD1	Leyland	72120		L27/24R	07/31	11/51	I.H 01/56 Oil engine inst. 08/46
2	TF5919	Leyland Titan TD1	Leyland	72121		L27/24R	07/31	11/51	I.H 05/53 2.S
3	TF5920	Leyland Titan TD1	Leyland	72122		L27/24R	07/31	11/51	I.H 01/56 2.S Oil engine inst. 11/49
8	TJ2813	Leyland Beaver TSC9	)# =	3374			09/33	05/51	I.W 09/60 2.S
11	TJ31	Leyland Bull TSQ3	*/)Leyland	227			01/34	--/41	I.W 09/40 2.F 5.V/D 12/32 * Hinged sides when new

Fleet No	Reg No	Chassis Type	Chassis No	Body Type	Body No	Seating	Date In	Date Out	Notes
9	TJ4391	Leyland Beaver TSC9	4223	*/) Platform)& Cab			02/34	05/51	I.W 12/60
10	TJ3991	Leyland Beaver TSC9	4253				02/34	05/51	I.W 12/61
4	ATD774	Leyland Titan TD4	9257	Ld/Burlingham		L27/24R	12/35	07/57	I.Sh 09/61 Oil engine inst. 11/53
5	ATD775	Leyland Titan TD4	9258	Ld/Burlingham		L27/24R	12/35	07/57	I.W 07/61 Oil engine inst. 07/50
6	ATD776	Leyland Titan TD4	9259	Ld/Burlingham		L27/24R	12/35	11/51	I.H 12/58 Oil engine inst. 11/46 Re-bodied L27/26R --/53
18	CTC267	Leyland Titan TD5	14213	Burlingham		L27/26R	08/37	02/58	I.H 03/59 2.w/d 08/62 Oil engine inst. 04/47
19	CTC268	Leyland Titan TD5	14214	Burlingham		L27/26R	08/37	02/58	I.Sh 09/63 2.w/d 12/66 Oil engine inst. 02/46
20	CTC269	Leyland Titan TD5	14215	Burlingham		L27/26R	08/37	02/58	2.S 05/59 Oil engine inst. 03/46
21	CTC270	Leyland Titan TD5	14216	Burlingham		L27/26R	08/37	02/58	2.S 05/59
28	DTE457	Leyland Lion LT9	302236	Leyland		B35F	01/39	10/57	2.WDV --/39 to --/45, S/Bu 03/60. Coach seats inst. --/--
29	DTE458	Leyland Lion LT9	302237	Leyland		B35F	01/39	12/56	I.H 09/61 2.w/d 10/65
30	DTE459	Leyland Lion LT9	302238	Leyland		B35F	01/39	07/54	I.H 09/59 2.w/d 01/63
31	DTE460	Leyland Lion LT9	302239	Leyland		B35F	01/39	07/54	I.H 05/59 2.w/d 12/62
7	GTD598	Leyland Tiger PS1	461049	Burlingham	2600	B34F	09/46	08/57	I.Sh --/-- 2.Bu 10/60
11	GTE395	Leyland Tiger PS1	461160	Burlingham	2601	B34F	10/46	09/57	I.Sh --/--
32	GTF282	Leyland Titan PD1 A	461659	Leyland		H30/26R	12/46	10/63	I.H --/64
33	GTF283	Leyland Titan PD1 A	461660	Leyland		H30/26R	12/46	11/64	I.H --/64
8	HTE954	Leyland Tiger PS1	462125	Burlingham	2405	B35F	08/47	07/57	I.Sh --/--
15	HTE955	Leyland Tiger PS1	462661	Burlingham	2406	B35F	09/47	08/57	I.Sh --/--
25	JTJ823	Leyland Titan PD2/1	484969	Leyland		H56R	02/49	10/66	Re-numbered 36 28/05/66
26	JTJ824	Leyland Titan PD2/1	490595	Leyland		H56R	02/49	10/66	2.S 01/66
24	KTJ482	Leyland Tiger PS1/1	493300	Burlingham	2698	B35F	10/49	09/63	I.H 01/65
34	KTJ481	Leyland Tiger PS1/1	493299	Burlingham	2699	B35F	10/49	09/58	I.H --/--
23	LTD445	Leyland Titan PD2/1	494247	Leyland		L27/26R	01/50	01/64	2.S 02/64
9	MTD513	Leyland Olympic HR44	504420	MCW	L80	B44F	03/51	11/70	I.H
10	MTD514	Leyland Olympic HR44	504421	MCW	L81	B44F	03/51	11/70	
22	MTD515	Leyland Olympic HR44	504419	MCW	L82	B44F	04/51	01/69	2.Bu 01-06/69 New 02/51
27	MTD516	Leyland Olympic HR44	511551	MCW	L83	B44F	07/51	11/70	
12	NTC231	Leyland Olympic HR44	511550	MCW	L87	B44F	07/51	01/70	2.Bu 06/72
13	NTC232	Leyland Olympic HR44	511673	MCW	L88	B44F	10/51	11/70	2.Ru/S 11/70
16	NTC233	Leyland Olympic HR40	511672	MCW	L89	B40F	10/51	12/70	2.Ru/S 12/70
17	NTC234	Leyland Olympic HR40	511549	MCW	L90	B40F	10/51	09/72	2.Ru/S 09/72 New 07/51
1	NTD423	Leyland Titan PD2/12	514529	Leyland		L27/26R	11/51	10/66	2.Dlr
2	NTD424	Leyland Titan PD2/12	514531	Leyland		L27/26R	11/51	06/66	2.Dlr
3	NTD425	Leyland Titan PD2/12	514530	Leyland		L27/26R	11/51	06/66	2.Dlr
6	TTB973	Leyland Titan PD2/12	532209	Leyland		H30/26R	08/54	08/72	2.w/d 08/73 S 02/74
14	TTB974	Leyland Titan PD2/12	532512	Leyland		H30/26R	08/54	07/69	2.w/d 02/73
7	521CTF	Leyland Olympian	576695	Weymann	LW47	B44F	11/57	03/73	2.P 05/93
8	522CTF	Leyland Olympian	576696	Weymann	LW48	B44F	11/57	03/73	2.Dlr 06/84 Re-reg JTF350B --/--
11	523CTF	Leyland Olympian	576697	Weymann	LW49	B40F	11/57	01/75	2.S 06/82
15	525CTF	Leyland Olympian	576699	Weymann	LW51	B44F	11/57	10/74	2.w/d --/77
28	524CTF	Leyland Olympian	576698	Weymann	LW50	B40F	11/57	01/75	2.w/d 12/77
29	526CTF	Leyland Olympian	576700	Weymann	LW52	B44F	11/57	10/75	2.Mc 05/81
4	527CTF	Leyland Titan PD2/40	573883	Weymann	M7830	L30/28R	03/58	08/74	2.w/d 03/76 Bu --/76
5	528CTF	Leyland Titan PD2/40	573884	Weymann	M7831	L30/28R	03/58	03/78	2.P 03/92
18	529CTF	Leyland Titan PD2/40	573886	Weymann	M7835	L30/28R	03/58	05/74	2.w/d --/75
19	530CTF	Leyland Titan PD2/40	573899	Weymann	M7833	L30/28R	03/58	05/74	2.w/d --/75

Fleet No	Reg No	Chassis Type	Chassis No	Body Type	Body No	Seating	Date In	Date Out	Notes
20	531CTF	Leyland Titan PD2/40	573926	Weymann	M7832	L30/28R	03/58	11/72	2.Dlr 01/76 Bu --/00
21	532CTF	Leyland Titan PD2/40	573927	Weymann	M7834	L30/28R	03/58	08/74	5.V/Pr --/62
C1	7587TF	Leyland Leopard PSU3/3RT	L01388	Duple Dragonfly	I33/I	C49C	05/63	10/75	New 11/06/63
C2	7588TF	Albion Victor VT21L	7810J	Duple Firefly	I43/13	C41F	07/63	06/73	New 14/06/63
C3	7589TF	Albion Victor VT21L	7811H	Duple Firefly	I43/14	C41F	07/63	06/73	2.F --/-- S 09/80
24	ATB596A	Leyland Atlantean PDR1/1 MkII	629717	MCW/Weymann	M1023	L39/34F	10/63	02/76	2.St 08/81 Bu 11/85
30	ATB597A	Leyland Atlantean PDR1/1 MkII	629730	MCW/Weymann	M1024	L39/34F	10/63	02/79	2.w/d 01/83 S 03/83
31	ATB598A	Leyland Atlantean PDR1/1 MkII	629731	MCW/Weymann	M1022	L39/34F	10/63	02/77	2.w/d 06/79
32	ATB599A	Leyland Atlantean PDR1/1 MkII	629734	MCW/Weymann	M1025	L39/34F	10/63	02/77	Orig. B53F up to 1970/71
11	CTB951B	Leyland Leopard PSU3/4R	L03124	MCW/Weymann	M1404	B49F	01/64	03/78	Orig. B53F up to 1970/71
28	CTB952B	Leyland Leopard PSU3/4R	L03125	MCW/Weymann	M1403	B49F	01/64	06/77	2.Dlr 12/80 S --/--
23	CTE442B	Leyland Atlantean PDR1/1MKII	L03181	MCW/Weymann	M1405	L39/34F	02/64	01/80	5.V/D (Glasgow) --/62 6. 06/63
34	SGD669	Leyland Atlantean PDR1/1	623350	Alexander	7080	H44/34F	03/65	02/76	2.Dlr 09/82
C6	RTD432C	Leyland Leopard PSU3/4RT	L41479	Duple Commander	163/62	C49F	10/65	08/77	2.w/d --/-- S 02/88
33	STC359C	Leyland Leopard PSU3/4RT	L41478	MCW/Weymann	M1896	DP49F	12/65	02/81	)Body numbers allocated by Operated in Canada
25	TTE641D	Leyland Atlantean PDR1/1	L43632	MCW	(M1893)	L39/31F	05/66	01/81	)Weymann but as mainly built Operated in Canada
35	TTE643D	Leyland Atlantean PDR1/1	L43634	MCW	(M1894)	L39/31F	05/66	01/81	)MCW numbers not carried. 2.F --/83 S --/--
26	TTE642D	Leyland Atlantean PDR1/1	L43633	MCW	(M1895)	L39/31F	06/66	01/81	
C7	XTB188D	Leyland Leopard PSU4/4RT	L60780	Plaxton Panorama	669746	C41F	07/66	11/77	2.Dlr 08/86 S --/--
C9	750TJ	Leyland Leopard PSU3/3RT	L01054	Duple Dragonfly	133/2	C49C	07/66	10/75	5.V/D --/62
C8	YTC794D	Bedford J2 SZ 10	6826796	Duple -Willowbrook	CFJ2/383	C19/20F	09/66	10/70	2.S --/--
2	YTE951D	Leyland Tiger Cub PSUC1/12	L70319	Massey	2689	B45F	11/66	01/78	
3	YTE952D	Leyland Tiger Cub PSUC1/12	L70320	Massey	2690	B45F	12/66	03/78	2.w/d 08/85Dlr 03/87 S --/--
C10	FTC550F	Austin J2 – M16	I5898I	Fineline Walker		C12F	10/67	05/72	
C11	LTE286F	Ford Transit BC O5HR	42697FE	Fowler		C12F	08/68	10/77	2.w/d 07/85 still owned 05/86 New 06/03/68
1	JTJ667F	Leyland Panther PSUR1/1R	700019	PRV	55973	B48F + 22st	04/69	11/78	2.S --/-- 5.V/D --/68 Orig B48D
12	VTD441H	Leyland Tiger Cub PSUC1/12	950120	Fowler		B44F	01/70	04/78	2.P 01/91
C4	VTC715H	Leyland Leopard PSU4A/4R	903333	Plaxton Panorama Elite	709088	C41F	03/70	11/81	2.BD 09/83
C5	VTC716H	Leyland Leopard PSU4A/4R	903334	Plaxton Panorama Elite	709089	C41F	03/70	07/82	Re-reg ABM61A II/84
13	BTD778J	Leyland Leopard PSU4A/2R	903107	Fowler		B44F	11/70	02/81	2.Dlr 11/83 S --/--
27	BTD780J	Leyland Leopard PSU4A/2R	903109	Fowler		B44F	11/70	02/81	2.Bu 01/83 S 08/83
16	BTD779J	Leyland Leopard PSU4A/2R	903108	Fowler		B44F	12/70	11/81	2.Dlr 11/83 S --/-- New 03/11/70
C8	MTC993K	Leyland Leopard PSU3B/4R	7101824	Plaxton Panorama Elite	729727	C49F	06/72	02/83	2.Dlr 09/90 S --/--
6	MTE186K	Leyland Atlantean PDR1/3	900579	Fowler		H43/30F	08/72	11/78	2.Dlr 07/83 Ws --/-- Chassis built 1969
17	STD179L	Leyland Atlantean AN68/1R	7201352	East Lancs	7207	H43/31F	10/72	01/83	2.w/d c01/02
9	WTE484L	Daimler Fleetline SRL6 – 36	66029	Fowler		B48F + 20st	03/73	10/79	2.w/d 12/82 S --/--
10	WTE485L	Daimler Fleetline SRL6 – 36	66030	Fowler		B48F + 20st	03/73	10/79	2.w/d 12/82 S --/--
C2	BTB778L	Leyland Leopard PSU3B/4RT	7300938	Plaxton Panorama Elite	733585	C49F	06/73	02/85	2.w/d --/96 St --/96 P?
C3	BTB779L	Leyland Leopard PSU3B/4RT	7300939	Plaxton Panorama Elite	733586	C49F	06/73	11/84	2.Dlr 11/95 S --/-- Re-reg R01990 04/95, SCK558L 07/91
7	TTJ496M	Daimler Fleetline SRL6 – 36	66031	Fowler		B48F + 20st	05/74	01/80	2.w/d 12/82 Bu/Dlr 01/84
8	TTJ497M	Daimler Fleetline SRL6 – 36	66032	Fowler		B48F + 20st	05/74	01/80	2.w/d 12/82 Dlr 01/84 S --/--
20	TTJ498M	Daimler Fleetline SRL6 – 36	66033	Fowler		B48F + 20st	08/74	09/80	2.Bu 09/80 S 11/80
18	XTB728N	Leyland Atlantean AN68/1R	7402342	East Lancs	2901	H43/31F	08/74	06/97	2.P 06/97 7. 03/89 – 09/90
19	XTB729N	Leyland Atlantean AN68/1R	7402386	East Lancs	2902	H43/31F	08/74	06/97	2.P 06/97 7. 03/89 – 09/90
4	HCW761N	Leyland National I II351A/1R	1897	LN		B49F + 24st	01/75	10/90	2.Dlr 03/96 S 8.a 02/84
21	HCW762N	Leyland National I II351A/1R	1898	LN		B49F + 24st	01/75	04/91	2.Dlr 08/96 S 8.b 02/87
C1	VUB398H	Leyland Leopard PSU3A/4R	7000938	Plaxton Panorama Elite	709189	C53F	11/75	03/78	2.Dlr 03/86 S --/-- 3.WA new 04/70 4.ST
C9	VUB400H	Leyland Leopard PSU3A/4R	7000836	Plaxton Panorama Elite	709187	C53F	11/75	03/78	2.S 02/88 3.WA new 04/70 4.ST

FLEET LIST - 4

Fleet No	Reg No	Chassis Type	Chassis No	Body Type	Body No	Seating	Date In	Date Out	Notes
14	PCK193P	Leyland National 1 11351A/1R	2891	LN		B49F+24st	01/76	10/91	2.w/d 04/98 S 07/98 8.b 01/86
22	SRN103P	Leyland Atlantean AN68/1R	7601727	East Lancs	6301	H43/32F	06/76	03/07	7.05/98 --/99, 01/01 - 07/03
15	NRN838P	Leyland National 1 11351A/1R	2725	LN		B49F+24st	02/77	10/86	2.w/d A Ru 10/86 S 12/86 6.10/75 to 01/77 8.a 01/84
29	XCW956R	Leyland National 1 11351A/1R	4119	LN		B49F+24st	02/77	04/91	2.S 05/02 7.04/91 – 11/93 Re-reg PIB8076 2.S 05/02
34	XCW957R	Leyland National 1 11351A/1R	4120	LN		B49F+24st	02/77	03/07	7.10/93 to 06/94 + 05/98 to --/99 + 04/01 to 09/01 8.b 04/86 9.06/94
C6	AHG947R	Leyland Leopard PSU3E/4R	7700103	Plaxton Supreme	7711LC109	C53F	06/77	03/86	8.d 01/84
C7	AHG948R	Leyland Leopard PSU3E/4R	7700386	Plaxton Supreme	7711LC110	C53F	07/77	04/86	2.S 02/02 8.d --/84 Re-reg 7622WF 03/93, AHG948R 01/98
28	FBV524S	Leyland National 1 11351A/1R	4846	LN		B49F+24st	12/77	03/07	7.05/98 to --/99 + 04/01 to 09/01 + 08/02 to 03/03 8.b 01/87 9.12/94
24	XCW955R	Leyland National 1 11351A/1R	4118	LN		B49F+24st	01/78	12/99	2.P 12/99 6.a 01/77 to 01/78 7.05/95 to 12/99 8.a 11/84
C9	GRN259S	Leyland Leopard PSU3E/4R	7705134	Plaxton Supreme	7811LC059	C53F	03/78	04/89	8.d 02/85 Re-reg 7586VM 10/90, IIL7921 02/95
2	PTC122M	Leyland National 1 1051/1R/0102	922	LN		B41F+20st	04/78	11/82	2.F/S --/-- 3/4.L new 01/74
5	PTC124M	Leyland National 1 1051/1R/0102	924	LN		B41F+20st	04/78	11/82	2.w/d 12/93 S 01/94. 3/4.L new 01/74
3	PTC123M	Leyland National 1 1051/1R/0102	923	LN		B41F+20st	04/78	04/82	2.w/Da 19/04/82 St/Ru 05/85 3/4.L new 12/73
31	FBV525S	Leyland National 1 11351A/1R	4924	LN		B49F+24st	01/79	03/92	New 23/12/77 2.w/d / S 12/01 6.a 01/78 to 01/79 7.03/92 to 11/93 8.b 06/86
6	NFR559T	Leyland National 1 11351A/1R	5758	LN		B49F+24st	01/79	03/07	7.05/98 to --/99 + 04/01 - 09/01 + 03/03 9.01/95 8.b 02/86 9.01/95
11	NFR560T	Leyland National 1 11351A/1R	5761	LN		B49F+24st	01/79	03/07	2.S 01/05 7.10/93 to 09/94 + 05/98 to --/99 + 04/0 to 09/01 +08/02 to 03/03 8.b 03/86 9.09/94
C1	OCK452T	Leyland Leopard PSU3E/4R	7802074	Plaxton Supreme IV Express	7911LX501	C53F	02/79	04/89	2.BDII/95 8.d 02/85 Re-reg JIL4653 07/94, HWR449T 12/95
1	NFR558T	Leyland National 1 11351A/1R	5757	LN		B49F+24st	01/80	05/95	2.dis/S 05/02 6.a 01/79 – 01/80 7.05/95 - 04/01 8.b 05/86
9	WRN412V	Leyland National 2 NLII6ALII/1R	6662	LN		B49F+24st	01/80		2.w/d(A) 12/04,Dis/St 06/05, 7.12/04 to 06/05 8.c 01/86
C10	XFR842V	Leyland Leopard PSU5C/4R	7902398	Duple Dominant II	35.5422	C57F	02/80	02/89	2.Bu/S 02/00 Re-reg 1862HX 07/92
20	FHG592S	Leyland Titan B15	7405999	Leyland/PRV		H47/26F	03/80	02/87	5. VPr/D --/74 (BI502) First reg --/77
25	NHG732P	Leyland Titan B15	7600668	Leyland/PRV	60769	H44/27F	09/80	04/84	5. VPr/D --/76 (BI504) Orig H44/27D,
C11	GCK431W	Leyland Leopard PSU5D/5R	7930139	Duple Dominant II	135.542	C57F	01/81	02/89	Conv H45/32F --/-- Re-reg UJI6314 06/96 2.S by 01/05 Re-reg 81 G 479 04/93
10	WRN413V	Leyland National 2 NLII6ALII/1R	6667	LN		B49F+24st	02/81	03/07	2.Dis/ S 11/03. 6.a 01/80 to 01/81. 7.10/03 to date 8.c --/88
7	GCK428W	Leyland National 2 NLII6ALII/1R	7343	LN		B49F+24st	02/81		8.c --/--
8	GCK429W	Leyland National 2 NLII6ALII/1R	7344	LN		B49F+24st	02/81		8.c --/--,
23	GRN895W	Leyland Atlantean AN69A/1R	7504065	ECW	24761	H43/31F	02/81		5.CT/Pr --/75 7.11/88 to 09/90
13	TLS733P	Leyland National 1 1095I/1R	431	LN		B49F+24st	08/81	05/82	Orig DP43D 4.R 09/02/81 5.VPr 02/73 8.c 09/86
16	OFV620X	Leyland National 2 NLII6ALII/1R	7599	LN		B49F+24st	01/81		New 10/02/81 2.Dis/St 09/05,S 18/10/06 6.a 03/81 to 01/82
12	GCK430W	Leyland National 2 NLII6ALII/1R	7345	LN		B49F+24st	02/82	06/07	8.c --/--
26	OFV621X	Leyland National 2 NLII6ALII/1R	7600	LN		B49F+24st	06/82		6.a 01/82 to 06/82 10.a 09/94to10/96 New 10/12/81
C4	TRN91X	Leyland Tiger 245 TRCTLII/3R	8200263	Plaxton Viewmaster IV	8212LTV4C912	C51F	07/82	02/89	Re-reg HSVI26 10/91, BUA7IIX 09/92 5. VPr/D --/77 (BI505) 2.P 08/96 Orig H44/27D.
3	BCK706R	Leyland Titan B15	7705689	Leyland/PRV	60770	H44/27F	12/82	11/86	Re-reg VLIT240 --/--, TMR535R --/--, BCK706R 05/97

Fleet No	Reg No	Chassis Type	Chassis No	Body Type	Body No	Seating	Date In	Date Out	Notes
C5	LSB83	Leyland Tiger 245 TRCTL11/3R	8200273	Plaxton Paramount 3500	8312LTH1C902	C51F	03/83	03/90	Re-reg FFV582Y 03/90, VIA451I 06/90, RCA151Y 09/05
27	ABV939Y	Leyland National 2 NL116ATL11/1R	7668	LN		B49F+24st	06/83	05/07	2.w/d 01/05, Dis/S 06/05. 6.a 01/83 to 06/83 7. 01/05 to 06/05, 8.c --/--
2	A462LFV	Leyland Atlantean AN69/2R	7801729	ECW	25310	H47/35F+8st	01/84	03/90	Orig AN69/2LSP Aqd 05/81 5.CT/Pr --/78 7.05/98 to --/99
C8	B350CJX	DAF MB200 DKFL600 XLACEO2LT 002	36016	Plaxton Paramount 3500	8512DZH2C754	C53F	06/85	02/86	11.b Re-reg TIL5402 04/01 2S by 09/05
C2	VKY43	Leyland Tiger 245 TRCTL11/3RH	8500069	Plaxton Paramount 3500	8512LZH2C782	C51F	07/85	11/90	11.b Re-reg B366DBV 11/90, HIL8436 03/92, A20SOE 05/99, 85 C 4479 03/03
C3	B894CFV	Leyland Tiger 245 TRCTL11/3RH	8500070	Plaxton Paramount 3500	8512LZH2C783	C51F	07/85	11/90	Re-reg LSB83 03/90, D378DBV 11/90, WDM193 04/91, J638JAB 01/95. Re-std C49FT 01/95
C6	C791MVH	DAF MB200 DKFL600 XLACEO2LT 002	36678	Plaxton Paramount 3500	8512DZH2C763	C53F	04/86	02/87	11.b Re-reg 86DLI1 05/87
C7	C792MVH	DAF MB200 DKFL600 XLACEO8LT 002	34647	Plaxton Paramount 3500	8512DZH2C765	C53F	04/86	03/87	11.b Re-reg LIL5069 07/95 2S by --/02
C8	C752MFR	Leyland Royal Tiger	RTC8605	Doyen — Leyland		C48FT	04/86	04/88	11.c Re-reg MIB526 11/90
C12	C753MFR	Leyland Royal Tiger	RTC8606	Doyen — Leyland		C48FT	04/86	04/88	11.c
25	D25VCW	Leyland Lynx LX112TL11ZR1	LX1031	LN		B47F+21st	12/86	04/07	Re-reg 86C4605 12/04
30	D30VCW	Leyland Lynx LX112TL11ZR1	LX1032	LN		B47F+21st	12/86	04/07	Re-reg 86C4606 12/04
C6	D274XCX	DAF SB2205 XLA DE23 H500 DHS 585	286411	Van Hool Alizee	12929	C55F	03/87	02/88	11.b Re-reg 5516PP 11/89, D397EDX 11/91, HIL8426 04/92 Re-std C51FT by 02/94
C7	D27SXCX	DAF MB230 DKFL615 XLACEO2LT 002	288445	Van Hool Alizee	12944	C55F	03/87	02/88	11.b Re-reg O1W711S 02/94. Re-std C53F by 09/94, C57F 07/03
C14	D276XCX	DAF MB230 DKFL615 XLACEO2LT 002	286578	Van Hool Alizee	12950	C55F	03/87	02/88	11.b Re-reg NIJ9479 02/92. Re-std C49FT 03/95, C55F 06/99, C49FT by 06/03
C15	D277XCX	DAF MB230 DKFL615 XLACEO2LT 002	288431	Van Hool Alizee	12945	C55F	03/87	02/88	11.b Re-reg NIW2320 03/94 Re-std C57F 05/02
C16	D619VCX	DAF SB2205 XLA DE23H 500 FHS 585	285933	Van Hool Alizee	12926	C55F	05/87	03/88	11.b Re-reg LS84I1 04/90, D98SGSG 01/93, YIL1845 06/04. Re-std C51F 12/96, C51FT 02/03
32	D32YCW	Leyland Lynx LX112TL11ZR1	LX1051	LN		B47F+21st	05/87	04/07	2.w/d 01/04
33	D33YCW	Leyland Lynx LX112TL11ZR1	LX1053	LN		B47F+21st	06/87	04/07	
M1	D703HUA	Freight Rover Sherpa 350D	255214	Optare	44	B16F+2st	06/87	03/89	2.w/d 03/97 Dlr 06/98 3.YR 09/86 4.YR Re-reg AOR947A 02/91, DI54CFR 06/92
M2	D711HUA	Freight Rover Sherpa 350D	256750	Optare	33	B16F+2st	06/87	03/89	2.Bu 06/97 So 3.YR 09/86 4.YR
M3	D704HUA	Freight Rover Sherpa 350D	256265	Optare		B16F+2st	07/87	03/89	3.YR 09/86 4.YR Re-reg RB7429S by 09/97, D704HUA by 12/01
M4	D712HUA	Freight Rover Sherpa 350D	256755	Optare	37	B16F+2st	08/87	03/89	2.w/d A 04/97 S 01/01 3.YR 09/86 4.YR
D	D319PDM	Iveco Ford F7,49-10	1182	Reeve Burgess	18565		07/87	09/87	11.e
M5	E45HBV	Mercedes Benz 609D 668063.20	814541	Reeve Burgess	16682	B20F+6st	09/87	09/00	8.e 06/98
M6	E46HBV	Mercedes Benz 609D 668063.20	816047	Reeve Burgess	16797	B20F+6st	09/87	10/00	8.e 09/98 Re-reg TIL5084 10/00, E46HBV 05/04
M7	E47HBV	Mercedes Benz 609D 668063.20	817091	Reeve Burgess	16798	B20F+6st	09/87	09/01	8.e 08/98
M8	D84BLF	Mercedes Benz 709D 669063.20	761918	Reeve Burgess	16416	C19F+6st	10/87	09/00	New 10/86 6.b 8.e 07/98 Re-reg TIL 5415 07/02
D	E106SOG	Freight Rover					11/87	12/87	11.e
C6	E346EVH	DAF SB3000 DKV601 XLA DA 32K 500	299244	Van Hool Alizee	13291	C55FT	02/88	12/88	11.b Re-reg A17ETL 07/01 Re-std C55F 04/97, C51FT 01/02
C7	E347EVH	DAF SB3000 DKV601 XLA DA 32K 500	299246	Van Hool Alizee	13292	C55FT	02/88	01/89	11.b Re-reg 613WHT 01/94, E347EVH 03/05, YIL8772 04/05. Re-std C55F by 03/96, C51FT by 01/02
C12	E349EVH	DAF SB3000 DKV601 XLA DA32K 500	299251	Van Hool Alizee	13296	C55FT	02/88	12/88	11.b Re-reg LS84I1 01/93, E668UMS 08/93, A14HJT 12/93, F08933 06/01, E227AUJ 08/06
C14	E320EVH	DAF 230LB DKFL 615 XLACEO 2LT 002	93161	Van Hool Alizee	13256	C55FT	02/88	12/88	11.b Re-reg A6YET 05/95, E689LBT 06/00. Re-std C53F 05/04
C16	E116KFV	Leyland Tiger 260 TRCTL11/3ARZ	TR00135	Plaxton Paramount 3500	8812LUH3C755	C51FT	02/88	02/90	11.a Re-reg JCN822 04/91, E116KFV 12/97, O1W1660 04/98
C17	E117KFV	Leyland Tiger 260 TRCTL11/3ARZ	TR00136	Plaxton Paramount 3500	8812LUH3C754	C51FT	02/88	02/90	11.a Re-reg 88DL4148 05/95
M9	D2100KY	Mercedes Benz 709D 669063.20	747814	Reeve Burgess	17222	B20F+6st	03/88	09/95	New 10/86 6.b
C8	E348EVH	DAF SB3000 DKV601 XLA DA32K 500	299250	Van Hool Alizee	13295	C55FT	03/88	12/88	11.b Re-reg GDZ571 04/96, E165WCL c08/97. Re-std C53F 04/04

FLEET LIST - 6

Fleet No	Reg No	Chassis Type	Chassis No	Body Type	Body No	Seating	Date In	Date Out	Notes
C15	E343EVH	DAF 230LB DKFL 615 XLACEO 2LT 002	9931l	Van Hool Alizee	13265	C55F	02/88	01/89	II.b Re-reg B7AND 02/96, E343EVH 04/97. Re-std C55FT 05/97
C18	E118KFV	Leyland Tiger 260 TRCTL11/3ARZ	TR00261	Plaxton Paramount 3500	8812LUH3C756	C51FT	04/88	04/90	II.a Re-reg SCL17 --/93?, 530MUY 03/97, E118KFV 06/06
C19	E119KFV	Leyland Tiger 260 TRCTL11/3ARZ	TR00258	Plaxton Paramount 3500	8812LUH3C757	C51FT	04/88	10/90	II.a Re-reg OIL3926 04/98
M10	E100MFV	Mercedes Benz 609D 668063.20	865456	Reeve Burgess	16949	C19F	05/88	05/07	8.e 05/98 7. --/ 04 05/07
C10	F550YCW	Bova FHD12/290	4193	Futura		C49FT	02/89	12/91	2.S --/99 Re-reg RJI8681 10/94.
C6	F56YCW	Leyland Tiger 260 TRCTL11/3ARZ	TR00662	Plaxton Paramount 3500	8912LFB 1475	C55F	03/89	03/92	II.a Re-reg NIL7044 07/97. Re-std C53F 07/96, C55F by03/02
C7	F57YCW	Leyland Tiger 260 TRCTL11/3ARZ	TR00664	Plaxton Paramount 3500	8912LFB 1476	C55F	03/89	03/92	II.a Re-reg S24FUP 06/92, EIBI647 10/97, F57YCW 12/97.
C8	F58YCW	Leyland Tiger 260 TRCTL11/3ARZ	TR00665	Plaxton Paramount 3500	8912LFB 1477	C49FT	03/89	03/92	Re-std C53F by 08/94, C50FT 01/96 II.a Re-reg 32CHY 12/95, F58YCW 02/01, BJZI383 02/02. Re-std C51F by 11/97, C49F 02/01
C9	F59YCW	Leyland Tiger 260 TRCTL11/3ARZ	TR00666	Plaxton Paramount 3500	8912LFB 1478	C49FT	03/89	03/92	II.a Re-reg 865EYT 11/95, F59YCW 02/01, LIB7134 04/01, F59YCW 06/03. Re-std C53F 07/02, C49FT 09/04
M1	F705WFV	Mercedes Benz 609D 668063.20	875782	Reeve Burgess	17073	C19F	03/89	09/01	8.e 08/98
M2	F706WFV	Mercedes Benz 609D 668063.20	878117	Reeve Burgess	16988	C19F	03/89	09/01	8.e 07/98
C1	F40BFR	Bova FHD12/290	4272	Futura		C49FT	04/89	12/91	Re-reg RJI8685 10/94
D	F792DWT	DAF		Optare			07/89	07/89	II.e
C3	G23MHG	Volvo B10M – 60 YV31MGD 10KA	21612	Van Hool Alizee	13912	C53F/49FT	03/90	03/95	II.a Re-reg BSK789 11/95, G23MHG 01/00, 90WD2208 04/02
C2	G22MHG	Volvo B10M – 60 YV31MGD 10KA	21613	Van Hool Alizee	13913	C53F/49FT	03/90	04/95	II.a Re-reg MBZ8505 09/95,YSV608 03/97, G264JSC 12 98, LUI 1729 08/02, XIL 3210 08/03. Re-std C49F 01/95, C55F 05/02
C4	G24MHG	Leyland Tiger TRCLI0/3ARZM	TR00638	Plaxton Paramount 3500	9012LCB 988	C51FT	03/90	03/93	II.a Re-reg FSU372 02/96, G24MHG 12/97, YUU556 05/98, G24MHG 02/01, 90KK3366 02/01.
C5	G25MHG	Leyland Tiger TRCLI0/3ARZM	TR00617	Plaxton Paramount 3500	9012LCB 990	C49FT	04/90	03/93	Re-std C49F 03/ 96, C51F by 01/01, C55F 02/01. II.a Re-reg FSU394 08/95, G25MHG 12/97, 583TD 06/98, G25MHG 02/01, NIL2460 04/01, G25MHG by 05/03, 98DL6262 by 08/03. Re-std C49F 03/96, C51F 07/02
4	F972HGE	Volvo B10M – 60 MkIII	20815	Plaxton Paramount 3500	8912VCB 1270	C53F/49FT	03/91	11/91	New 03/89 .3.PH. II.a Re-reg AI6BUS 04/92
	F973HGE	Volvo B10M – 60 MkIII	20816	Plaxton Paramount 3500	8912VCB 1271	C53F/49FT	04/91	11/91	New 03/89. 3.PH. II.a Re-reg JSK261 01/93, F973HGE 10/05
	H64CCK	Leyland Lynx 2 LX2R11C15Z4R	LX2040	LN		B47F+22st	04/91	01/07	10.a 03/97 to 03/00? 2. W/d -Dis 09/05, S 01/07 7.
5	H65CCK	Leyland Lynx 2 LX2R11C15Z4R	LX2041	LN		B47F+22st	04/91		14/09/05 to19/01/07
3	J7JFS	Leyland Lynx 2 LX2R11C15Z4R	LX2043	LN	30544	B47F+22st	10/91	10/95	II.b Re-reg JI58OHG 01/95, I482PP by --/ 02, J9130PV 02/06, AI6LKR 03/06.
	J9JFS	DAF SB3000DKFV601 XLV DE33K TOH	309	Van Hool Alizee MkIV		C49FT	03/92		
	G53RGG	Volvo B10M – 60 MkIII	22817	Plaxton Paramount 3500	9012VCB 1488	C53F/49FT	03/92	02/95	New 03/90. 3.PH. II.a Re-reg C49F 01 95, C53F 05/00
	G54RGG	Volvo B10M – 60 MkIII	22814	Plaxton Paramount 3500	9012VCB 1489	C53F/49FT	03/92	02/95	New 03/90. 3.PH. II.a Re-reg GSU230 by 08/ 98, G54RGG 10/01. Re-std C49F by01/95.
	G55RGG	Volvo B10M – 60 MkIII	22896	Plaxton Paramount 3500	9012VCB 1490	C53F/49FT	03/92	02/95	New 03/90. 3.PH. II.a Re-reg IKZ3291 06/02. Re-std C49F by 01/95, C53F 08/95, C49FT 02/01, C57F 10/03
	G56RGG	Volvo B10M – 60 MkIII	22898	Plaxton Paramount 3500	9012VCB 1491	C53F/49FT	03/92	02/95	New 03/90. 3.PH. II.a Re-reg USVI15 01/98, G56RGG 11/02.
I4	J14JFS	Leyland Lynx 2 LX2R11C15Z4R	LX2044	LN		B47F+22st	03/92	10/92	Re-std C49F By 01/95, C53F by 06/97, C57 --/05
	J796KHD	DAF MB230LT615 XLRCE02LT0E	32S329	Van Hool Alizee MkIII	30565	C51FT/55F	05/92		II.b Re-leased 05/93 to 10/93. Re-std C53F 11/00, C55F by 10/02
	K3JFS	Volvo B10M – 60 YV31MGD10 MS	25741	Plaxton Premiere	9112VCP 0362	C49FT	03/93	04/95	II.a Re-reg K624FEC 01/95, ACY911 02/03 (Malta)
	K4JFS	Volvo B10M – 60 YV31MGD19 NA	29763	Plaxton Premiere	9112VCP 0137	C49FT	03/93	04/95	II.a Re-reg K623FEC 01/95, K5STMT 02/03.
	K5JFS	Mercedes Benz 814 6703132N	9714	Autobus Classique MkII Plaxton Pointer	1082	C29F	05/93 --/93	05/95 --/93	Re-std C50F by 05/96 Orig reg K721GBE. Re-reg K721GBE 08/02 II.e

Fleet No	Reg No	Chassis Type	Chassis No	Body Type	Body No	Seating	Date In	Date Out	Notes
D	KS10RJX	DAF		Ikarus			--/93	--/93	II.e
15	UMR194T	Daimler Fleetline FE30AGR	7802384	ECW	23475	H43/31F	11/93	07/97	New 02/10/78 4.Th
17	UMR196T	Daimler Fleetline FE30AGR	7802386	ECW	23478	H43/31F	02/94	07/97	New 01/11/78 4.Th
D	L829HEF	Volvo B10B		Alexander			03/94	03/94	II.e
D	L416PAR	Dennis Dart		Marshall			03/94	03/94	II.e
	LIJF5	EOS E180Z YA 9CF 2G27 RB	128960	EOS 90	R9/8960	C49FT	04/94	04/97	II.b Re-reg L347LCK 04/97, G1GLT 08/02
	K531RJX	DAF SB3000DKFV601 XLV DE33K TOH	2911	Van Hool Alizee MkIV	31468	C51FT	05/94	08/94	New 03/93 II.b
20	LUA714V	Bristol VRT SL3/6LXB	2200	ECW	23905	H43/31F	07/94	11/00	New 19/02/80 3.WY 4.NB
21	DWU295T	Bristol VRT SL3/6LXB	1623	ECW	23379	H43/31F	07/94	10/00	New 01/11/78 3.WY 4.NB
	M823RCP	EOS E180Z YA 9CF 2G24 RB	128107	EOS 90	R9/8107	C48FT	01/95	02/98	Built 27/09/94 II.b/D
21	K3JF5	DAF SB3000WS XLV DE33W SOH	4274	Van Hool Alizee MkIV	31965	C51FT	03/95	10/97	10.b until 06/96 II.b Re-reg M818WEO 10/97, JIL7889 --/00, M818WEO 11/03
	J9JF5	EOS E180Z YA 9CF 2G22 SB	128130	EOS 90	S9/8130	C48FT	03/95	04/98	II.b Re-reg M569ACK 04/98
D	M21UUA	Optare		Sigma			03/95	03/95	II.e
	M664WCK	Volvo B10M — 62 YV31 M2B 19SA	42630	Plaxton Excalibur	9512VUS 2993	C49FT	04/95	04/00	II.a Re-reg KBZ 1487 06/02, M664WCK 02/03, LUI7662 03/03, M664WCK 04/05.
	M665WCK	Volvo B10M — 62 YV31 M2B 10SA	42631	Plaxton Excalibur	9512VUS 2998	C49FT	04/95	04/00	10.c 1995 Season II.a Re-reg KBZ 1410 07/02, M665WCK 02/03, LUI7668 03/03.
	N662KCW	EOS E180Z YA 9CF 2H26 SB	128162	EOS 90	S9/8162	C49FT	03/96	04/99	Built 09/95 II.b/D
	N985FWT	DAF SB3000WS XLV DE33W SOH	5002	Van Hool Alizee MkIV	32802	C49FT	05/96	05/99	II.b 10.b Re-reg 770HDM by 05/06
STL1	M822RCP	DAF SB220 LT550 XLVDE02LTOH	3989	Northern Counties	4803	B49F+22St	09/96	03/97	II.b
STL13	M850RCP	DAF SB220 LT550 XLVDE02LTOH	4012	Northern Counties	4811	B49F+22St	09/96	03/97	II.b Re-reg YAZ 4143 --/01
	P866PWW	DAF SB3000WS XMG DE33W SOH	5606	Van Hool Alizee MkV	32833	C49FT	04/97	05/00	II.b 10.b Re-reg 294DDM 02/03
	P867PWW	DAF SB3000WS XMG DE33W SOH	5607	Van Hool Alizee MkV	32834	C49FT	04/97	10/00	II.b 10.b
15	R845VEC	Dennis Dart SLF SFD 322BR1VGW	10933	Wright Crusader	Y239	}	07/97		
17	R846VEC	Dennis Dart SLF SFD 322BR1VGW	10934	Wright Crusader	Y236	} B41(37)F	07/97		
18	R847VEC	Dennis Dart SLF SFD 322BR1VGW	11126	Wright Crusader	Y238	} +20(24)St	07/97		
19	R848VEC	Dennis Dart SLF SFD 322BR1VGW	11127	Wright Crusader	Y237	}	07/97		
29	AAP651T	Bristol VRT SL3/6LXB	1662	ECW	Y238	H43/31F	08/97	11/00	New 06/12/78 3.Sd 4.C
	HJB461W	Bristol VRT SL3/6LXB	2707	ECW	Y239	H43/31F	08/97	12/00	New 17/11/80 3.AV 4.C
31	R61GNW	DAF SB3000WS XMG DE33W SOH	5598	Van Hool Alizee T9	Y240	C48FT	04/98	01/01	II.d/D Released 07-08/01 + 09-10/01 + 09-10/02, Re-std C49FT II/02. Re-reg SEL73 by 009/06
	R62GNW	DAF SB3000WS XMG DE33W SOH	6244	Van Hool Alizee T9	Y241	C48FT	04/98	10/01	II.d 10.b Re-std C49FT II/02 Re-reg SEL36 02/06
	T58AUA	DAF SB3000WS XMG DE33W SOH	7145	Van Hool Alizee T9	Y242	C48FT	04/99	10/02	II.d Re-std C49FT II/02 Re-reg SEL23 02/06
	T57AUA	DAF SB3000WS XMG DE33W SOH	6390	Van Hool Alizee MkV	Y243	C49FT	05/99	10/02	II.d 10.b Re-std C48FT T04/03
13	EAP988V	Bristol VRT SL3/6LXB	2241	ECW	Y244	H43/31F	10/99	11/00	New 14/03/80 3.Sd 4.Src/S, Reinst — OS door inst'd, Re-std H43/27F. Re-reg NCS437G --/--
24	LFJ879W	Bristol VRT SL3/6LXC	2833	ECW	Y245	H43/31F	10/99	10/00	New 01/03/80 3.WN 4.Src/UC
D	T290ROF	Volvo B6BLE		Wright Crusader			11/99	11/99	II.e
STL1	M844RCP	DAF SB220 LT550 XLVDE02LTOH	3973	Northern Counties	4797	B49F+22St	02/00	05/00	II.d Re-reg KUI 9266 06/01
	W223CDN	EOS E180Z YA 9CF 2N28 YB	180650	EOS 90 / Van Hool	Y/80650	C48FT	04/00	11/04	II.d
	W224CDN	EOS E180Z YA 9CF 2N2X YB	180651	EOS 90 / Van Hool	Y/80651	C48FT	04/00	11/03	II.d Re-reg 179BUT 06/06
1	LIJF5	DAF SB120 LF XMGDEI2CSOH	7561	Wright Cadet	B241	B42F+11St	05/00		Built 09/99
21	UHG144V	Leyland Atlantean AN68A/2R	7902673	Alexander	AL83/1777/2	H49/36F	10/00	09/04	New 03/80 3.PB, 4. PB 7. 04/04 2. Dis/S
24	UHG148V	Leyland Atlantean AN68A/2R	7902831	Alexander	AL83/1777/8	H49/36F	11/00	02/07	New 03/80 3.PB, 4. PB, 2. w/d 10/06, S 02/07
35	R32GNW	DAF SB220 GS XMGDE02GSOH	5468	Northern Counties	5612	B41F+27St	11/00	11/04	II.d 4.A 03/01
STL36	M848RCP	DAF SB220 LT550 XLVDE02LTOH	4010	Northern Counties	4809	B49F+22St	11/00	02/01	II.d Re-reg PAZ9346 05/02
13	UHG147V	Leyland Atlantean AN68A/2R	7902828	Alexander	AL83/1777/6	H49/36F	11/00	10/06	II.d Re-reg 03/80 3.PB, 4. PB 2.S 19/10/06

FLEET LIST - 8

Fleet No	Reg No	Chassis Type	Chassis No	Body Type	Body No	Seating	Date In	Date Out	Notes
20	UHG150V	Leyland Atlantean AN68A/2R	7903227	Alexander	AL83/1777/10	H49/36F	12/00	02/07	New 03/80 3.PB. 4. PB 2.S 28/02/07
22	UHG149V	Leyland Atlantean AN68A/2R	7902834	Alexander	AL83/1777/7	H49/36F	01/01	02/07	New 03/80 3.PB. 4. PB 2 S 01/03/07
36	X821NWX	DAF SB120 LF XMGDE12CSOH	8741	Wright Cadet	D467	B42F+11St	02/01		
38	X823NWX	DAF SB120 LF XMGDE12CSOH	8743	Wright Cadet	D469	B42F+11St	02/01		
37	X822NWX	DAF SB120 LF XMGDE12CSOH	8742	Wright Cadet	D468	B42F+11St	02/01		
	Y477HUA	EOS E180Z YA 9CF 2N20 YB	180660	EOS 90/Van Hool	X/80660	C49FT	03/01	04/04	11.d Released 20 - 24/09/04
	Y478HUA	EOS E180Z YA 9CF 2N2X XB	180647	EOS 90/Van Hool	X/80647	C49FT	03/01	04/04	11.d, 10.b
29	T154AUA	Mercedes Benz T814D 670373.2N0	75362	Alexander	9720/34	B33F	08/01	03/05	4.A 7. 12/04 to 02/05
	YD02RHF	EOS E180Z YA 9CF 2N29 YB	180656	EOS 90/Van Hool	X/80656	C49FT/51	02/02	10/05	11.d Orig reg YJ 51ENT
D	YD02RDY	DAF SB200 LF XMGDE02CSOH	9633	Wright Commander	E66	B44F+28St	05/02	05/02	11.e Ret 03/03 to 04/03 (Rept for 40)
STL	T182AUA	EOS E180Z YA 9CF 2N24 WB	180075	EOS 90/Van Hool	W/80075	C48FT	06/02	06/02	11.d
39	YG52EVY	DAF SB200 LF XMGDE02CSOH	9435	Wright Commander	F316	B44F+29St	08/02		
40	YG52CFY	DAF SB200 LF XMGDE02CSOH	9568	Wright Commander	F317	B44F+29St	08/02		
STL	W188CDN	EOS E180Z YA 9CF 2N25 YB	180654	EOS 90/Van Hool	Y/80654	C51FT	12/02	01/03	New 04/00 11.d
	YJ03PDU	DAF SB4000XF XMGDE40X SOH	9654	Van Hool Alizee T9	37037	C42FT	03/03	01/07	11.d
	YJ03PDV	DAF SB4000XF XMGDE40X SOH	10278	Van Hool Alizee T9	37036	C42FT	03/03	01/07	11.d
41	YJ03PFG	DAF SB200 LF XMGDE02CSOH	10345	Wright Commander	F726	B44F+29St	03/03		
42	YJ03PFF	DAF SB200 LF XMGDE02CSOH	10344	Wright Commander	F725	B44F+29St	03/03		
STL	R82GNW	EOS E180Z YA 9CF 2N24 TB	180007	EOS 90/Van Hool	T/80007	C48FT	09/03	10/03	New 04/98 11.d
10	YJ53VDT	DAF SB200 LF XMGDE02CSOH	10244	Wright Commander	F720	B44F+29St	01/04		
11	YJ53VDV	DAF SB200 LF XMGDE02CSOH	10245	Wright Commander	F721	B44F+29St	02/04		
	YJ04BJF	DAF SB4000XF XMGDE40X SOH	10991	Van Hool Alizee T9	37078	C42FT	02/04		11.d
	YJ04BYG	DAF SB4000XF XMGDE40X SOH	10993	Van Hool Alizee T9	37080	C36FT	02/04		11.d
	YJ04BYF	DAF SB4000XF XMGDE40X SOH	10992	Van Hool Alizee T9	37079	C36FT	02/04	02/06	11.d Re-std C41FT 03/04
34	F355WSC	Leyland ONCL10/2RZ	11137	Alexander	RH62/5088/17	H81F+15St	09/04		New 04/89 3. Ln, 4. Ln Conv SD 10/04
32	F352WSC	Leyland ONCL10/2RZ	11134	Alexander	RH62/5088/2	H81F+15St	09/04		New 04/89 3. Ln, 4. Ln Conv SD 10/04
33	F353WSC	Leyland ONCL10/2RZ	11135	Alexander	RH62/5088/3	H81F+15St	10/04		New 04/89 3. Ln, 4. Ln Conv SD 10/04
9	YJ54CFM	DAF SB120 BS XMGDE12BSOH	11961	Wright Cadet	H575	B39F+23St	12/04		11.d Initially No 6, changed to No 9 01/02/05
6	YJ54CFN	DAF SB120 BS XMGDE12BSOH	11953	Wright Cadet	H576	B39F+23St	12/04		11.d Initially No 9, changed to No 6 01/02/05
	YD05PWN	DAF SB4000XF XMGDE40X SOH	11945	Van Hool Alizee T9	37116	C42FT	03/05		11.d
28	YJ55KZP	DAF SB200 LF XMGDE02CSOH	12438	Wright Commander	J725	B44F+29St	09/05		
29	YJ55KZR	DAF SB200 LF XMGDE02CSOH	12439	Wright Commander	J726	B44F+29St	09/05		
	YJ06LGA	DAF SB4000XF XMGDE40X SOH	13511	Van Hool Alizee T9	37161	C42FT	03/06		11.d
30	G802GSX	Leyland ONCL10/2RZ	11487	Alexander	RH75/3088/3	H81F+15St	09/06		New 04/90 3. Ln, 4. Ln Conv SD & Re-std H84F 10/06
31	G806GSX	Leyland ONCL10/2RZ	11491	Alexander	RH75/3088/7	H81F+15St	09/06		New 04/90 3. Ln, 4. Ln Conv SD & Re-std H84F 10/06
24	YJ07JWD	DAF SB200 LF XMGDE02CSOH	13510	Plaxton Centro	06 119 LBA 6403	B45F+26St	02/07		
25	YJ07JWE	DAF SB200 LF XMGDE02CSOH	14611	Plaxton Centro	06 119 LBA 6835	B45F+26St	03/07		
	YJ07JWF	DAF SB4000XF XMGDE40X SOH	14373	Van Hool Alizee T9	37192	C42FT	02/07		
	YJ07JWG	DAF SB4000XF XMGDE40X SOH	14454	Van Hool Alizee T9	37193	C42FT	02/07		
STL50	YJ07JDZ	DAF SB200 LF XMGDE02CSOH	14163	Wright Commander	AA252	B44F+29St	03/07	04/07	Built 09/06. Rept for 41
D	BX56VTP	Mercedes WEB6280802311092 6		Citaro		B41F+28St	04/07		11.e

John Fishwick & Sons   FLEET LIST NOTES

I.   LAST REGISTERED AS:

H — Hackney	Pr — Private	Sh — Showman's	W — Wagon	Wt — Wagon and trailer

2.   STATUS:

Am — Used as Ambulance	S — Scrapped	Bu — Broken up	P — Preserved	Sc — Noted as stationary caravan
BD — Converted to breakdown vehicle	St — Used as store	Dis — Dismantled	W — Converted to wagon	Dlr — Sold to dealer/ Other Operator
WDV — Used by War Dept.	F — Destroyed by fire	Ws — Used as a workshop	Hc — Used as hen cabin	w/d — Withdrawn
w/d(A) — Withdrawn after accident	Ru — Running units removed / body scrapped		Mc — Used as mobil caravan	

3.   ORIGINALLY ORDERED BY / REGISTERED TO:

AV — Alder Valley	B — Bridges Motor Serv	E — Eccleston Motor Co	L — Lancaster Corp Trans
Ln — Lothian	PB - Preston Bus	PH — Parks of Hamilton	Pn — Parkinson
Sd — Southdown	Th — Thamesdown	WA — Wallace Arnold	WN -— Western National
WY — West Yorkshire	Y — Yarrow Motor Co	YR — Yorkshire Rider	

4.   AQUIRED FROM:

A — Arriva	C - Claireaux of Hadleigh	L - Lancaster Corp Tran	Ln - Lothian	PB - Preston Bus
Th — Thamesdown	NB - Northern Bus of Anston	YR - Yorkshire Ride	ST - Smiths of Tysoe	Y - Yarrows Motor Co
R - Rennies of Dunfermline	Stc/S - Stagecoach, South	Stc/UC - Stagecoach, United Counties		

5.   BUILT BY LEYLAND AS CHASSIS — C / VEHICLE — V FOR:

T — Test	Pr — Prototype	D — Demonstration

6.   USED AS DEMONSTRATION VEHICLE PRIOR TO ENTERING SERVICE WITH FISHWICK.

a. Leyland   b. Mercedes Benz / Reeves Burgess

7.   PLACED IN STORE AT CHAPEL BROW.

8.   RECEIVED REVISED LIVERY / FLEETNAMES;

a. JOHN FISHWICK AND SONS and JFS scroll on front

b. John Fishwick and sons and JFS scroll on front

c. John Fishwick and sons

d. Revised coach livery

e. Revised minibus livery — FISHKWICK deleted

9.   CONVERTED TO DAF ENGINE / VENTILATION MODIFICATIONS BY HUGHES DAF.

10.   LIVERY ALTERATIONS:

a. All over advertisement

b. Leger livery

c. Four Seasons livery

II.   LEASED / DEMONSTRATION FROM DEALER:

a. Kirby Bus and Coach

b. Hughes DAF / D — used by dealer as Demonstrator prior to delivery

c. Leyland Bus

d. Arriva

e. Demonstration

WAGONS

No	Reg
1	John Fishwick
2	Steam Wagon
4	?
6	B5783 #
5	B5951 #
7	B8631
17	TC6272
20	TD5016
21	TD7271
22	TE1014
8	TJ2813
9	TJ4391
10	TJ3991
11	TJ31

MINIBUSES

No	Reg
M1	D703HUA *
M2	D711HUA
M3	D704HUA *
M4	D712HUA
M5	E45HBV
M6	E46HBV *
M7	E47HBV
M8	D84BLF *
M9	D210OKY
M10	E100MFV
M1	F705WFV
M2	F706WFV

BUSES

No	Reg	No	Reg	No	Reg	No	Reg
3	B2247	23	LTD445	15	NRN838P	13	UHG147V
5	B55.. or B23..	9	MTD513	17	SRN103P	20	UHG150V
8	B8851	10	MTD514	14	PCK193P	22	UHG149V
9	)	22	MTD515	24	XCW955R	36	X821NWX
10	) TB3775	27	MTD516	29	XCW956R *	38	X823NWX
11	TB6627	12	NTC231	34	XCW957R	37	X822NWX
12	TB7414	13	NTC232	28	FBV524S	29	T154AUA
13	TC5847	16	NTC233	31	FBV525S	39	YG52EVY
14	TC5874	17	NTC234	2	PTC122M	40	YG52CFY
15	TC6O53	1	NTD423	3	PTC123M	41	YJ03PFG
16	TC6093	2	NTD424	5	PTC124M	42	YJ03PFF
18	TD5014	3	NTD425	1	NFR558T	10	YJ53VDT
19	TD5O15	6	TTB973	6	NFR559T	11	YJ53VDV
20	TE1637 (a)	14	TTB974	11	NFR560T	34	F355WSC
21	TE1636	7	521CTF	9	WRN412V	32	F352WSC
22	TE1695	8	522CTF *	10	WRN413V	33	F353WSC
23	TE1694	11	523CTF (d)	13	TLS733P	9	YJ54CFM
24	TE1834	28	524CTF (e)	7	GCK428W	6	YJ54CFN
25	TE2331	15	525CTF	8	GCK429W	28	YJ55KZP
26	TE2332	29	526CTF	12	GCK430W	29	YJ55KZR
9	TE4619	4	527CTF	23	GRN895W	30	G802GSX
10	TE4620	5	528CTF	16	OFV620X	31	G806GSX
11	TE4621	18	529CTF	26	OFV621X	24	YJ07JWD
15	TE4622	19	530CTF	27	ABV939Y	25	YJ07JWE
12	TE7865	20	531 CTF	20	FHG592S	50	YJ07JDZ
13	TE7862	21	532CTF	25	NHG732P *		
14	TE7863	24	ATB596A	3	BCK706R *		
16	TE7864	30	ATB597A	2	A462LFV		
17	TE9307	31	ATB598A	25	D25VCW		
5	TD97O3 (b)	32	ATB599A	30	D30VCW *		
6	TE909	11	CTB951B	32	D32YCW *		
7	TE1998	28	CTB952B	33	D33YCW		
8	TE1794	23	CTE442B	4	H64CCK		
1	TF5921	34	SGD669	5	H65CCK		
2	TF5919	33	STC359C	3	J7JFS		
3	TF5920	25	TTE641D	14	J14JFS		
4	ATD774	26	TTE642D	15	UMR194T		
5	ATD775	35	TTE643D	17	UMR196T		
6	ATD776	2	YTE951D	20	LUA714V		
18	CTC267	3	YTE952D	21	DWU295T		
19	CTC268	1	JTJ667F	1	M822RCP		
20	CTC269	12	VTD441H	13	M850RCP *		
21	CTC270	13	BTD778J	15	R845VEC		
28	DTE457	16	BTD779J	17	R846VEC		
29	DTE458	27	BTD780J	18	R847VEC		
30	DTE459	6	MTE186K	19	R848VEC		
31	DTE460	17	STD179L	29	AAP651T		
7	GTD598	9	WTE434L	31	HJB461W		
11	GTE395	10	WTE4S5L	13	EAP988V		
32	GTF282	7	TTJ496M	24	LFJ879W		
33	GTF283	8	TTJ497M	1	M844RCP *		
8	HTE954	20	TTJ49SM	1	L1JFS		
15	HTE955	18	XTB728N	21	UHG144V		
25	JTJ823 (c)	19	XTB729N	24	UHG14SV		
26	JTJ824	4	HCW761N	35	R32GNW		
24	KTJ482	21	HCW762N	36	M848RCP *		
34	KTJ481						

COACHES

No	Reg	No	Reg
C1	7587TF	(C11)	F972HGE *
C2	7588TF	(C12)	F973HGE *
C3	7589TF	(C1)	J9JFS *
C6	RTD432C	(C6)	G53RGG *
C7	XTB188D	(C7)	G54RGG *
C9	750TJ	(C8)	G55RGG *
C8	YTC794D	(C9)	G56RGG *
C10	FTD550F	(C10)	J796KHD
C11	LTE286F	(C5)	K3JFS *
C4	VTC715H *	(C4)	K4JFS *
C5	VTC716H	(C11)	K721GBE *
C8	MTC993K		L1JFS *
C2	BTB778L		K531RJX
C3	BTB779L *		M823RCP
C1	VUB398H		J9JFS *
C9	VUB400H		K3JFS *
C6	AHG947R		M664WCK *
C7	AHG948R *		M665WCK *
C9	GRN259S *		N662KCW
C1	OCK452T *		N985FWT *
C10	XFR842V *		P866PWW *
C11	GCK431W *		P867PWW
C4	TRN91X *		R61GNW *
C5	LSB83 *		R62GNW *
(C8)	B350CJX *		T58AUA *
C2	VKY43 *		T57AUA
C3	B894CFV *		W223CDN
C8	C752MFR *		W224CDN *
C12	C753MFR		Y477HUA
C6	C791MVH *		Y478HUA
C7	C792MVH *		YD02RHF
C6	D274XCX *		T182AUA
C7	D275XCX *		W188CDN
C14	D276XCX *		YJ03PDU
C15	D277XCX *		YJ03PDV
C16	D619YCX *		R82GNW *
C14	E320EVH *		YJ04BJF
C15	E343EVH *		YJ04BYG
C6	E346EVH *		YJ04BYF
C7	E347EVH *		YD05PWN
C8	E343EVH *		YJ06LGA
C12	E349EVH *		YJ07JWF
C16	E116KFV *		YJ07JWG
C17	E117KFV *		
C18	E118KFV *		
C19	E119KFV *		
(C6)	F56YCW *		
(C7)	F57YCW *		
(C8)	F58YCW *		
(C9)	F59YCW *		
(C1)	F40BFR *		
(C10)	F550YCW *		
(C2)	G22MHG *		
(C3)	G23MHG *		
(C4)	G24MHG *		
(C5)	G25MHG *		

NOTES

(a) became No 27
(b) became No 6 – wagon
(c) became No 36
(d) became No C4,14
(e) became No C5. 22

\# Convertible Wagon/Chara
* Vehicle re-registered
? Reg number not known

RE REGISTRATIONS OF VEHICLES OPERATED

ORIGINAL REGISTRATION	1	2	3	4	5	6	7
522CTF	JTF350B						
XCW956R	PIB8076						
NHG732P	UJI6314						
BCK706R	VLT240	TMX535R	BCK706R				
D25VCW	86C4605						
D30VCW	86C4606						
D32VCW	86WX????						
M844RCP	KUI9266						
GAP988V	NCS437G						
M850RCP	YAZ4143						
M848RCP	PAZ9346						
D703HUA	AOR947A	D154CFR					
D704HUA	RBZ4295	D704HUA					
D84BLF	TIL5415						
E46HBV	TIL5084	E46HBV					
VTC715H	ABM61A						
BTB779L	ROI990	SCK558L					
AHG948R	7662WF	AHG948R					
GRN259S	7586VM	IIL7921					
OCK452T	JIL4653	HWR449T					
XFR842V	1862HX						
GCK431W	81 G 479						
TRN91X	HSV126	BUA711X					
LSB83	FFV582Y	VIA4511	RCA151Y				
B350CJX	TIL5042						
VKY43	B366DBV	HIL8436	A20SOE	85C4479			
B894CFV	LSB83	B378DBV	WDM193	J638JAB			
C791MVH	86 DL 11						
C792MVH	LIL5069						
C752MFR	MIB526						
D274XCX	5516PP	D397EDX	HIL8426				
D275XCX	OIW7115						
D276XCX	NJI9479						
D277XCX	NIW2320						
D619YCX	LS8411	D985GSG	YIL1845				
E320EVH	A6YET	E689LBT					
E116KFV	JCN822	E116KFV	OIW1660				
E117KFV	88DL 4148						
E346EVH	A17ETL						
E347EVH	613WHT	E347EVH	YIL8772				
E349EVH	LS8411	E668UMS	A14 HJT	FO8933	E227AUJ		
E343EVH	B7AND	E343EVH					
E348EVH	GDZ571	E165WCL					
E118KFV	SCL17	530MUY	E118KFV				
E119KFV	OIL3926						
F550YCW	RJI8681						
F56YCW	NIL7044						
F57YCW	524FUP	EIB1647	F57YCW				
F58YCW	32CHY	F58YCW	BJZ1383				
F59YCW	865EYT	F59YCW	LIB7134	F59YCW			
F40BFR	RJI8685						
G23MHG	BSK789	G23MHG	90WD 2208				
G22MHG	MBZ5805	YSV608	G264JSC	LUI1729	XIL3210		
G24MHG	FSU372	G24MHG	YUU556	G24MHG	90KK 3366		
G25MHG	FSU394	G25MHG	583TD	G25MHG	NIL2460	G25MHG	98DL 6262
F972HGE	A16BUS						
F973HGE	JSK261	F973HGE					
J9JFS (SB3000) '92	J158OHG	I482PP	J913OPV				
G54RGG	GSU230	G54RGG					
G55RGG	IKZ3291						
G56RGG	USV115	G56RGG					
K3JFS (B10M) '93	K624SEC	K55TMT					
K4JFS (B10M) '93	K623SEC	ACY911					
K721GBE	K5JFS	K721GBE					
L1JFS (EOS) '94	L347LCK	G1GLT					
K3JFS (SB3000) '95	M818WEO	JIL7889	M818WEO				
J9JFS (EOS) '95	M569ACK						
M664WCK	KBZ1487	M664WCK	LUI7662	M664WCK			
M665WCK	KBZ1410	M665WCK	LUI7668				
N985FWT	770HDM						
P866PWW	294DDM						
R61GNW	SEL73						
R62GNW	SEL36						
T58AUA	SEL23						
W224CDN	179BUT						
YJ51ENT	YD02RHF						

SPECIAL REGISTRATIONS

LSB83*
(03/90)

'83 Leyland Tiger/Plaxton
'85 Leyland Tiger/Plaxton
(Transferred to family car)

VKY43*

'85 Leyland Tiger/Plaxton
(Transferred to family car)

J7JFS

'91 Leyland Lynx

J9JFS*

'92 DAF SB3000/Van Hool
'95 EOS 90

J14JFS

'92 Leyland Lynx

K3JFS*

'93 Volvo B10M/ Plaxton
'95 DAF SB3000/ Van Hool

K4JFS*

'93 Volvo B10M/ Plaxton
Transferred to company car

K5JFS*

'93 Mercedes T814/ Autobus Classique

LIJFS

'94 EOS 90
'00 DAF SB120/ Wright Cadet

*now not used

SUMMARY OF VEHICLES operated over 100 years

VEHICLE TYPE/ MAKE	WAGONS			BUSES						COACHES			TOTALS
				Single Deck		Double Deck		Mini	Midi	Full Size	Mini	Midi	
	Steam	Petrol	Diesel	Petrol	Diesel	Petrol	Diesel						
LEYLAND	1	8+1C	4	37	62	10	45			33			200
ALBION										2			2
BEDFORD											1		1
AUSTIN											1		1
FORD/IVECO								1D			1		1+1D
DIAMLER					5		2						7
DAF					17 3D 4STL					32			49+ 3D 4STL
FREIGHT ROVER								4 1D					4+ 1D
MERCEDES								8	1			1	10
BOVA										2			2
VOLVO					2D					12			12+2D
EOS										9 3STL			9+ 3STL
BRISTOL							6						6
DENNIS					4 2D								4+ 2D
OPTARE					1D								1D
TOTALS	1	8	4	37	88 4STL 8D	10	53	12 2D	1	90 3STL	3	1	**318 +11D**

NOTES   C – Conversion   D – Demonstration Vehicle   STL – Short Term Loan Vehicle

WAGONS
1 x LSWC Steam Wagon
8 x Leyland Wagon, Petrol Engine
4 x Leyland Wagon, Diesel Engine
1 x Leyland converted from PLSC Lion SD Bus   Sub Total 13

BUSES
SINGLE DECK
37 x Leyland, Petrol Engine
62 x Leyland, Diesel Engine
5 x Daimler
4 x Dennis
21 x DAF   (Inc 4 STL)   Sub Total 130
DEMONSTRATORS
3 x DAF, 2 x Dennis, 2 x Volvo, 1 x Optare   Sub Total 8
DOUBLE DECK
10 x Leyland, Petrol Engine
45 x Leyland, Diesel Engine
2 x Daimler
6 x Bristol   Sub Total 63

MINI BUSES
4 x Freight Rover
8 x Mercedes Benz   Sub Total 12
DEMONSTRATORS
1 x Iveco Ford, 1 x Freight Rover   Sub Total 2

MIDI BUSES
1 x Mercedes Benz   Sub Total 1

COACHES
FULL SIZE
2 x Albion
33 x Leyland
32 x DAF
2 x Bova
12 x Volvo
12 x EOS   (Inc 3 STL)   Sub Total 93
MINI
1 x Bedford
1 x Austin
1 x Ford   Sub Total 3
MIDI
1 x Mercedes   Sub Total 1

Total   318+11D

JOHN FISHWICK & SONS - CURRENT KNOWN STATUS OF VEHICLES OPERATED OVER 100 YEARS

Note: C - Store vehicle in yard

Fleet Reg. No	Reg. No	Last Known Status
2	Steam Wagon	S
3	B2247	S
4	?	S
5	B55..orB23..	S
6	B5783	S
5	B5951	S
7	B8631	S
8	B8851	S
9)	?	
10)	TB3775	S
11	TB6627	S
12	TB7414	S
13	TC5847	S
14	TC5874	S
15	TC6053	S
16	TC6093	S
17	TC6272	S
18	TD5014	S
19	TD5015	S
20	TD5016	S
21	TD7271	S
22	TE1014	S
20	TE1637	S
21	TE1636	S
22	TE1695	S
23	TE1694	S
24	TE1834	S
25	TE2331	S
26	TE2332	S
6	TE4619	S
9	TE4620	S
11	TE4621	Preserved – Mark Hayes
15	TE4622	S
8	TE7865	S
12	TE7862	S
13	TE7863	S
14	TE7864	S
29	TE9307	S
5	TD9703	Preserved – Bill Ashcroft
6	TE909	S
7	TE1998	S
8	TE1794	S
21	TF5921	S
2	TF5919	S
3	TF5920	S
11	TJ2813	S
1	TJ31	S
9	TJ4391	S
10	TJ3991	S
4	ATD774	S
5	ATD775	S
6	ATD776	S
18	CTC267	S
19	CTC268	S
20	RTD432C	S
21	STC359C	S
28	DTE457	Grayline, Victoria, Canada
35	DTE458	Chr'n Grp, Vancouver, Can.
26	DTE459	S
31	DTE460	S (Reg transferred to car)
7	GTD598	S
11	GTE395	S
32	GTF282	S
33	GTF283	S
8	HTE954	S
15	HTE955	S
25	JJ823	S
26	JJ824	Preserved – Mark Hayes
24	KTJ482	S
34	KTJ481	S
23	LTD445	S
9	MTD513	S
10	MTD514	S
22	MTD515	S
27	MTD516	S
22	MTC993K	S
27	MTE186K	S
12	STD179L	Howells, Deri, S W
9	WTE484L	S
16	WTE485L	S
17	BTB778L	S
1	BTB779L	S
7	TTJ496M	S
8	TTJ497M	S
20	TTJ498M	S
12	NTC231	S
13	NTC232	S
16	NTC233	S
17	NTC234	S
1	NTD423	S
2	NTD424	S
3	NTD425	S
6	TTB973	Preserved – Mark Hayes
14	TTB974	Preserved – Mark Hayes
18	XTB728N	S
19	XTB729N	S
4	HCW761N	S
21	HCW762N	S
15	VUB398H	S
29	VUB400H	S
22	PCKI93P	Mobile Music, Crooklands
4	SRN103P	S
5	NRN838P	Preserved – Bill Ashcroft
18	XCW956R	S
19	XCW957R	Church Group, Preston
20	AHG947R	S
21	AHG948R	S
28	FBV524S	Arla Foods, Leeds
24	XCW955R	Preserved – Bill Ashcroft
9	GRN259S	S
2	PTC122M	S
5	PTC124M	S
3	PTC123M	S
31	FBV525S	Arla Foods, Leeds
6	NFR559T	S
11	NFR560T	S
28	OCK452T	Pennine, Skipton
1	NFR558T	S
9	WRN412V	S
C10	XFR842V	?
20	FHG592S	People with a Mission, Perth
25	NHG732P	? Preservation
C11	GCK431W	S
10	WRN413V	S
7	GCK428W	S
8	GCK429W	S
23	GRN895W	S
13	TLS733P	S
16	0FV620X	S
12	GCK430W	S
26	0FV621X	S
1	TRN91X	S
C4	BCK706R	Scutt, Owston Ferry
C5	LSB83	Preserved – Mark Hayes
27	ABV939Y	Barratt, d/l Middlewich
2	A462LFV	S
(C8)	B350CJX	Lyons, Milltown Malbay SI
C2	VKY43	Stone, Edenbridge
C3	B894CFV	S
C6	C791MVH	S
C7	C792MVH	S
C8	C752MFR	Lloyds – Dlr, S on Trent
C12	C753MFR	Lakeland Comm, Kendal
25	D25YCW	PSV Products, Warrington
30	D30VCW	Kells Bus Museum, Cork, SI
C6	D274XCX	Dlr / Fin – Reposes
C7	D275XCX	Wigan Coachways, Wigan
C14	D276XCX	Cross Country, Swindon
C15	D277XCX	Wigan Coachways, Wigan
16	D619YCX	FreeBird, Bury
32	D32YCW	Brendon Edward, E'cthy, SI
33	D33YCW	Glenferry, Passage West, SI
M1	D703HUA	S
M2	D711HUA	S
M3	D704HUA	S
M4	D712HUA	S
M5	E45HBV	Star Travel, Aylesbury
M6	E46HBV	Oakleaf, Carlton
M7	E47HBV	Al Motors, Warrington
M8	D84BLF	?
C6	E346EVH	Elizabethan, Walsall
C7	E347EVH	TallyHo, Kingsbridge
C12	E349EVH	Worthern, Minsterley
C14	E320EVH	Fletcher, Burton
C16	E16KFV	Ribble Valley, Goosnargh
C17	E117KFV	Gallagher, Brinalack, NI
M9	D2I00KY	? SI / NI
C8	E348EVH	Bakers, Yeovil
C15	E343EVH	Mann, Gravesend
C18	E118KFV	
C19	E119KFV	Ace Travel, Brighton
M10	E100MFV	Private Owner, Manchester
C10	F550YCW	McAnulty, Warrenpoint NI
(C6)	F56YCW	Phoenix, Swindon
(C7)	F57YCW	S
(C8)	F58YCW	Rooney, Hilltown, NI
(C9)	F59YCW	? SI
M1	F705WFV	Kimberley, Low Prudoe
M2	F706WFV	Coffin, Church Crookham
(C1)	F40BFR	Fields, Tickhill
(C3)	G23MHG	Suirway, Passage East, SI
(C2)	G22MHG	Edwards, Llant Farde, SW
(C4)	G24MHG	Roberts, Myshall, SI
(C5)	G25MHG	Reddins, Muff, SI
C11	F972HGE	Wests, Woodford Green
C12	F973HGE	Roselyn, Parr
4	H64CCK	S
5	H65CCK	S
5	JJFS	S
(C1)	J9JFS	S
(C6)	G53RGG	Lamberts, Beccles
(C7)	G54RGG	Pearson, Chesterfield
(C8)	G55RGG	Rainbow, Billingham
(C9)	G56RGG	Mac Donald, Muirhead, Sc'd
4	J14JFS	Barrys, Weymouth
C10	J796KHD	Birmingham Coach, W Brom
(C11)	K3JFS	Supreme, Malta
15	K4JFS	S
(C11)	K721GBE	Assett, West Bromwich
15	UMRI94T	Globe, Barnsley
17	UMRI96T	S
	LIJFS	Film Unit, Co Gwy/Clare SI
	KS31RJX	Bretherton, Chipping
20	LUA714V	Donnelly, Grandard, SI
21	DWU29ST	Alphine, Llandudno
	M823RCP	S
	K3JFS	Leander, Swadlingcote
	J9JFS	Lutterworth, Lutterworth
	M664WCK	Rainbow, Billingham
	M65WCK	Premier, Nottingham
	N662KCW	Arriva, Dlr
	N985FWT	Jones, Flint
1	M822RCP	S
13	M850RCP	Ensign Dlr
	P866PWW	Kimes, Folkingham
	P867PWW	Jones, Flint
15	R845VEC	Geldards, Leeds
17	R846VEC	S
19	R847VEC	S
	R848VEC	S
29	AAP65IT	Alphine, Llandudno
31	HJB461W	Alphine, Llandudno
	R61GNW	Selwyns, Runcorn
	R62GNW	Selwyns, Runcorn
	T58AUA	Selwyns, Runcorn
	T57AUA	Geldards, Leeds
13	EAP988V	Autobus Gal'd, Quebec, Can
24	LF879W	S
1	M844RCP	K Line, Honley
	W223CDN	Arriva, Dlr
	W224CDN	Butler, Kirby in Ashfield
	LIJFS	C
21	UHGI44V	Kimes, Folkingham
24	UHGI48V	S
35	R32GNW	C
36	M848RCP	S
13	UHGI47V	Elite, Poulton
20	UHGI50V	S
22	UHGI49V	Arriva, Dlr
36	X821NWX	C
38	X823NWX	Arriva, Dlr
37	X822NWX	C
	Y477HUA	C
	Y478HUA	C
29	T154AUA	Arriva, Dlr
	YD02RHF	C
	T182AUA	C
39	YGS2EVY	C
40	YGS2CFY	C
	WI88CDN	Dewhirst, Bradford
	YJ03PDU	? South Wales
	YJ03PDV	Dalesman, Guisley
41	YJ03PFG	C
42	YJ03PFF	C
	R82GNW	BSS, Bolton
10	YJ53VDT	C
11	YJ53VDV	C
	YJ04BJF	C
	YJ04BYG	C
	YJ04BYF	C
34	F355WSC	Staintons, Kendal
32	F352WSC	C
33	F353WSC	C
9	YJ54CFM	C
6	YJ54CFN	C
	YD05PWN	C
28	YJ55KZP	C
29	YJ55KZR	C
	YJ06LGA	C
30	G802GSX	C
	G806GSX	C
24	YJ07JWD	C
	YJ07JWF	C
	YJ07JWG	C
25	YJ07JWE	C
50	YJ07JDZ	C

DEMONSTRATION VEHICLES LOANED

| REGISTRATION NUMBER | VEHICLE TYPE | | NUMBERS | | DATES |
	Chassis	Body	Chassis	Body	
D319PDM	Iveco Ford F7.49/10	Reeve Burgess	1182	18565	July 1987
E106SOG	Freight Rover	?			Nov/Dec 1987
F792DWT	DAF	Optare			July 1989
J120SPF	Dennis Lance	Plaxton Pointer			1993
K510RJX	DAF	Ikarus			1993
L829HEF	Volvo B10B	Alexander			June 1994
L416PAR	Dennis Dart	Marshall			March 1994
M21UUA	Optare	Sigma			March 1995
T290ROF	Volvo B6BLE	Wright Crusader			Nov/Dec 1999
YD02RDY	DAF	Wright Commander			17-24 May 2002
BX56VTP	Mercedes	Citaro			11-18 April 2007

T290ROF - Volvo B6BLE with Wright Crusader body

YD02RDY - DAF SB120 with Wright Commander body

BX56VTP - Mercedes Citaro

BREAKDOWN VEHICLES OPERATED

REGISTRATION	VEHICLE TYPE	DATES	NOTES
MTJ601C 218CK) Trade)Plate Q27GHG G837VHK	Ley TSC9 Beavers Austin Gypsy Bedford S Type Scammell Handyman Atkinson Borderer DAF 2500 - FT 2500 DHS 285	Mid 30's - Early 50's 20/04/65 - 09/12/72 --/--/-- - Mid 88 Mid 88 - Mid 99 Mid 99 - date	As required Also service vehicle Leyland Engine Leyland 680 Engine Cummins Engine Ch Type XLRTE25HSOE No 331109 First Reg 01/01/89

G837VHK   DAF 2500

SERVICE VEHICLES OPERATED

REGISTRATION	VEHICLE TYPE	DATES	NOTES
MTJ601C	Austin Gypsy	20/04/65 - 09/12/72	Passed to J C Brindle, Euxton
RTE697C	Austin Mini - van	20/10/65 - 30/09/68	
CTJ529E	Triumph Courier	28/04/67 - 23/04/70	
NBV385T	Austin Mini - van	--/--/79 - --/--/83	
KWC723Y	Ford Escort Van	--/--/83 - --/--/91	
G611UNB	Ford Transit Van	--/--/91 - --/02/00	
T436LBV	Ford Transit Van	--/02/00 - date	

ACKNOWLEDGEMENTS

The Author David Prescott would like to acknowledge the following:

Reference to publications:
Joint Bus Services between Leyland and Preston
Commercial Motor
The Leyland Journal
Leyland Bus by Doug Jack
Buses
Buses Extra

Information was also obtained from:
Lancashire Records Office
PSV Circle
Ribble Enthusiasts Club

Individuals I would like to thank are:
Mr J C Brindle
Mr J Hustler
Mr Cross of Fishwicks
Mr Alan Watson of Fishwicks
The late Mr A R (Tony) Bennison
The late Mr Don Threlfall
The late Mr Tim Mason
Mr Peter Hesketh
Mr John Madge
Mr Mike Sutcliffe
Mr Harold Preistley
Mr Geoff Meek and son James
Kath Bradshaw
And all individuals at Fishwicks who have assisted
in their various ways

A number of firms and organisations have cooperated with Bill Ashcroft and the Ribble Vehicle Preservation Trust to celebrate the Company's Centenary year and we would like to acknowledge their assistance and / or sponsorship. They include:

A K Stainless
Almar Services
Arriva Bus & Coach
Bosal (UK)
Campbells Caravans
C & W Berry Ltd
P.H. Chandler
Crossley's Metal Fabrications

Heatons Engineering Group
Holdens Commercial Vehicle
Services
Hoghton Timber
JKS Advertising
Joinery Design Ltd
Lancashire Football Association
Leyland Trucks

Life & Commercial Insurance
Brokers
National Westminster Bank
Roadferry
Simmal
Stagecoach
Whittle Flooring

Our Celebratory Open Day on Sunday 8th July 2007 will involve the members of the Friends of the Commercial Vehicle Museum, the Leyland Soceity, the Ribble Vehicle Preservation Trust and the staff of John Fishwick & Sons and we thank them all.

PHOTO CREDITS

THE AUTHOR

David Prescott was born in September 1947, served a trade apprenticeship at Leyland Motors and became an Engine Technician in the Research and Development Department, later becoming a Development Engineer on engines. Since 1993 he has been a coach driver on vintage and modern coaches. He has been interested in bus and coach type vehicles since school days and has spent the last 15 - 30 years-researching material for this publication. An interest in preservation resulted in the purchase of a 1961 Leyland Leopard/Harrington Cavalier ex-Ribble coach, which at present is still undergoing restoration. David is always on the look out for more information concerning the history of Fishwicks, its vehicles and employees, and would particularly welcome the loan for copying of any photographs, which would extend his collection. These would be returned promptly. He can be contacted either by post at 11 Brookside Road, Fulwood, Preston PR2 9TR or email: davidprescott1@btinternet.com